lonely planet

KT-239-281

# BARCELONA
## ENCOUNTER

**DAMIEN SIMONIS**

914·672

44191557

**Barcelona Encounter**

**Published by Lonely Planet Publications Pty Ltd**
ABN 36 005 607 983

| | |
|---|---|
| **Australia** | Head Office, |
| | Locked Bag 1, Footscray, Vic 3011 |
| | ☎ 03 8379 8000  fax 03 8379 8111 |
| | talk2us@lonelyplanet.com.au |
| **USA** | 150 Linden St, Oakland, CA 94607 |
| | ☎ 510 250 6400 |
| | toll free 800 275 8555 |
| | fax 510 893 8572 |
| | info@lonelyplanet.com |
| **UK** | 2nd fl, 186 City Rd |
| | London EC1V 2NT |
| | ☎ 020 7106 2100  fax 020 7106 2101 |
| | go@lonelyplanet.co.uk |

This title was commissioned in Lonely Planet's London office and produced by: **Commissioning Editors** Korina Miller, Clifton Wilkinson, Lucy Monie **Coordinating Editors** Charlotte Orr, Stephanie Pearson **Coordinating Cartographer** Julie Dodkins **Layout Designer** Carol Jackson **Assisting Editor** Barbara Delissen **Senior Editors** Helen Christinis, Katie Lynch **Managing Cartographer** Shahara Ahmed **Project Managers** Eoin Dunlevy, Fabrice Rocher **Language Content Coordinator** Quentin Frayne **Managing Layout Designer** Celia Wood **Thanks to** Glenn Beanland, Yvonne Bischofberger, Jessica Boland, Ryan Evans, Jennifer Garrett, Mark Griffiths, Jim Hsu, Laura Jane, James Hardy, Martin Heng, Lauren Hunt, Lisa Knights, Glenn van der Knijff, Alison Laming, Wayne Murphy, Trent Paton, Julie Sheridan, Lyahna Spencer

ISBN 978 1 74179 161 7

Printed through Colorcraft Ltd, Hong Kong.
Printed in China.

**Acknowledgement** Barcelona Metro Map © TMB 2008.

**Mixed Sources**
Product group from well-managed forests and other controlled sources
www.fsc.org  Cert no. SGS-COC-005002
© 1996 Forest Stewardship Council

FSC

# HOW TO USE THIS BOOK
## Colour-Coding & Maps

Colour-coding is used for symbols on maps and in the text that they relate to (eg all eating venues on the maps and in the text are given a green knife and fork symbol). Each neighbourhood also gets its own colour, and this is used down the edge of the page and throughout that neighbourhood section.

Shaded yellow areas on the maps denote 'areas of interest' – for their historical significance, their attractive architecture or their great bars and restaurants. We encourage you to head to these areas and just start exploring!

**Send us your feedback** We love to hear from readers — your comments help make our books better. We read every word you send us, and we always guarantee that your feedback goes straight to the appropriate authors. The most useful submissions are rewarded with a free book. To send us your updates and find out about Lonely Planet events, newsletters and travel news visit our award-winning website: *lonelyplanet.com/contact*.

Note: We may edit, reproduce and incorporate your comments in Lonely Planet products such as guidebooks, websites and digital products, so let us know if you don't want your comments reproduced or your name acknowledged. For a copy of our privacy policy visit *lonelyplanet.com/privacy*.

## DAMIEN SIMONIS

Damien occasionally steps onto the minuscule balcony of his Eixample flat and wonders by what stroke of fortune he wound up here. He has been in and out for years, watching Barcelona grow into one of Europe's most popular cities. It all started on a visit prior to the 1992 Olympics. Something hooked him that hasn't let go. For Damien, Barcelona is as close as possible to urban perfection.

## DAMIEN'S THANKS

Thanks to all those who have shared tips and company: Anna Arcarons, María Barbosa and Enric Muñoz, Sandra Canudas, Dominique Cerri, Paolo Cesco, Oscar Elias, Veronica Farré, Damien Harris, Ralf Himburg and Lilian Müller, Edith López, Soledad Moreiro, Teresa and Carlos, Niko von Mosch and co, Steven Muller and Veronika Brinkmann, Sonja Müller-Salget, Nicole Neuefeind, Susana Pellicer (with Albert and friends), David Poveda, John Rochlin (ASBA), Gemma Sesplugues, Peter Sotirakis, Armin Teichmann, José María Toro, Michael van Laake and Rocío Vázquez, Nuria Vilches and Simona Volonterio.

**Our readers** Many thanks to the travellers who wrote to us with helpful hints, useful advice and interesting anecdotes. Phill Clarke, Emma Donaldson, Matthew Ginnever, Eva Vicar, Kathryn Willcocks.

**Cover photograph** La Ribera neighbourhood, Barcelona by Antoine Tardy. This image was selected as one of the winners of a competition to find four unique travellers' photos that really convey the experience of using an Encounter guide. Entrants were challenged to submit eye-catching photos that get right to the heart of the city and give the impression of seeing and experiencing it for themselves. Check out the other winning images on London, Paris and Istanbul Encounter covers. **Internal photographs** p54, p71, p84, p120 by Damien Simonis; p15 Elan Fleisher/Photolibrary; p31 Gavin Gough/Alamy. All other photographs by Lonely Planet Images, and by Mark Avellino p23; Bethune Carmichael p45; Krzysztof Dydynski p8, p20, p21, p25, p34, p112, p162, p167, p168, p174, p177; John Elk III p17; Martin Hughes p65, p94, p108, p135, p171; John Hay p11; Dennis Johnson p26, Alfredo Maiquez p6, p22; Chris Mellor p27; Guy Moberly p6, p24, p28, p29, p37, p38, p48, p80, p101, p149; Martin Moos p19; Neil Setchfield p34, p53, p59, p73, p75, p79, p82, p139, p142, p150, p161, p165; Oliver Strewe p116; Barbara Van Zanten p4, p156; Sune Wendelboe p91; Brent Winebrenner p12, p33, p86. All images are copyright of the photographers unless otherwise indicated.

Many of the images in this guide are available for licensing from **Lonely Planet Images:** www.lonelyplanet images.com

Enjoy the moving music and fancy footwork of flamenco (p170)

# CONTENTS

Why is our travel information the best in the world? It's simple: our authors are passionate, dedicated travellers. They don't take freebies in exchange for positive coverage so you can be sure the advice you're given is impartial. They travel widely to all the popular spots, and off the beaten track. They don't research using just the internet or phone. They discover new places not included in any other guidebook. They personally visit thousands of hotels, restaurants, palaces, trails, galleries, temples and more. They speak with dozens of locals every day to make sure you get the kind of insider knowledge only a local could tell you. They take pride in getting all the details right, and in telling it how it is. Think you can do it? Find out how at **lonelyplanet.com**.

# THIS IS BARCELONA

Compact Barcelona is a bright, fiery star lapped by the Mediterranean, a magnet to everyone from art-loving beach bums to business execs with a weakness for sunny downtime. It's a city in motion, constantly reinventing itself.

Barcelona manages the trick of merging past with future into an effervescent present. At its core lies one of Europe's best-preserved Gothic-era medieval city centres. That priceless heritage lent Gaudí and Co the historical foundation and inspiration for some of their zaniest architectural creations centuries later. Their adventurousness is in the city's DNA – local and international architects continue to unleash their unfettered fantasies here. As a skyline symbol, Gaudí's La Sagrada Família has stiff competition in Jean Nouvel's shimmering Torre Agbar.

The heady mix of Gothic monuments and contemporary skyscrapers is accompanied by a bevy of world-class museums that take you from the wonders of giant Romanesque frescoes to the playfulness of Joan Miró, from pre-Columbian South American gold to early Picasso.

All that culture fuels the appetite and at times the entire city seems to be out to lunch (or dinner). Thousands of restaurants offer an incredible palette for the palate, from traditional Catalan cooking to the last word in 21st-century *nueva cocina española* kookiness. A plethora of tippling establishments and dance clubs also spreads in a hedonistic arc across the entire city. Drop into century-old taverns or glam it up in bright new seaside bars. Shoppers, meanwhile, may never make it to a museum. Phalanxes of one-off boutiques compete with armies of global-brand-name stores.

Barcelonins have a reputation for hard work, but everywhere you look people seem to be having fun. On the waterfront, Rollerbladers glide past domino-playing pensioners, sun-seekers, windsurfers and sailors. Skateboarders practise their art in motion outside the Macba, temple to contemporary creation, and mountain-bikers blaze trails in the Collserola park.

Barcelona is an intoxicating ride. Once is unlikely to be enough.

---

**Top** The Barri Gòtic (Gothic Quarter; p42) **Bottom** *Jamón* (cured ham) for sale in atmospheric Gràcia (p128)

# >HIGHLIGHTS

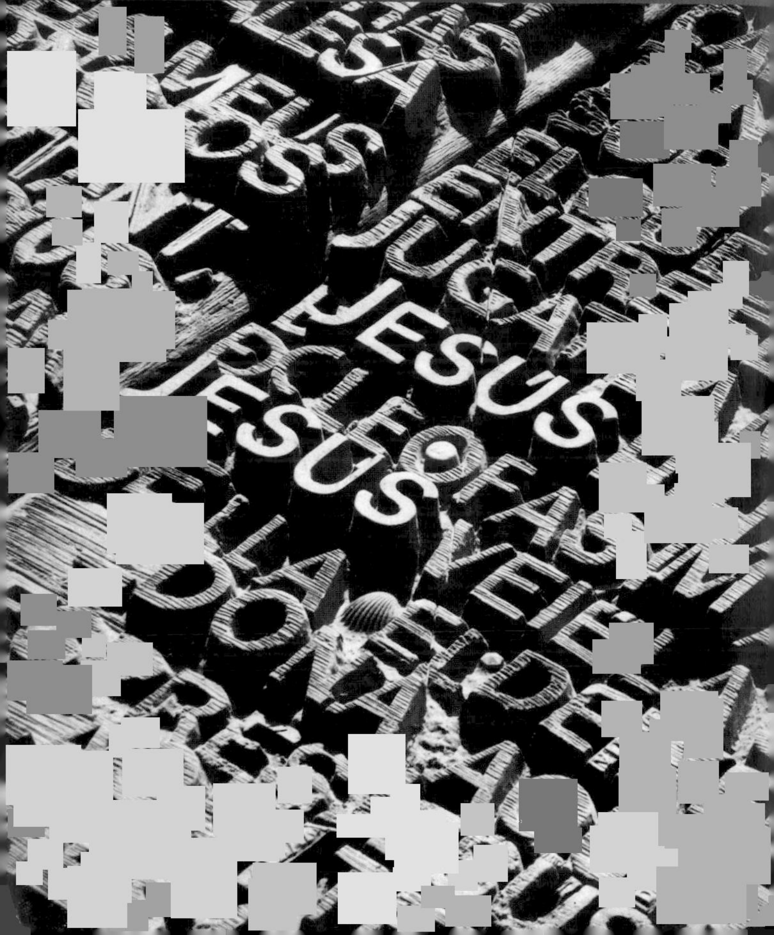

Bronze door detail in the Passion facade of Gaudí's La Sagrada Família (p110)

HIGHLIGHTS

# >1 LA SAGRADA FAMÍLIA

## SCALING THE DIZZY HEIGHTS OF LA SAGRADA FAMÍLIA

It is Spain's most visited sight – and the blinking thing isn't even finished! For many, that is part of the attraction. If you have been to Barcelona before, you have probably already visited Antoni Gaudí's La Sagrada Família church. But that was last time, wasn't it? A work in progress, it is never quite the same.

To enter La Sagrada Família is to crawl around inside one of the 20th century's most eccentric architectural minds. Gaudí planned three façades, dedicated to the Nativity (largely done in his lifetime), the Passion (finished in 1976) and the Glory; the last is the main one, on which work is now under way. Each is to be crowned by four towers, representing the 12 Apostles. Four higher towers will symbolise the Evangelists, while a colossal 170m-high central tower, flanked by another bearing a statue of the Virgin, will represent Christ.

There are two ways to experience the majesty of this divine construction site. The first is by looking upwards. The Nativity façade tells the story of Christ's birth and also represents the virtues of Faith, Hope and Charity. Local plant species and the nearby Montserrat mountain range inspired much of the curvaceous sculpture. The Passion façade also invites you to look skyward, following the story of Christ's passion and death. Inside the five-nave interior, you cannot fail to follow the sinewy lines of the forest of treelike pillars upwards, where they splay outwards in a canopy of concrete branches to hold up the roof.

Then you can do the opposite. Lifts and stairs allow you to ascend a tower of each façade and look down over the splendid work below

---

### BIRD'S-EYE VIEWS

More than two million visitors a year don't seem to bother the pair of peregrine falcons that nests high up in one of La Sagrada Família's towers. The last of these majestic birds living in Barcelona had been killed in 1973 but, since 1999, four pairs have been reintroduced, including this one with the rather exclusive address.

and the city around it, and perhaps feel a breath of the heavenly inspiration that touched Gaudí.

Get here as early in the morning as you can to avoid the worst of the crowds. Photography fans might want to turn up before opening time to catch the early sunlight on the exterior. An alternative is seeing it lit up at night (lights are usually out by midnight).

See p110 for more information.

# >2 LA RAMBLA

## TAKING THE CITY'S PULSE FROM ITS BUSIEST BOULEVARD, LA RAMBLA

Perhaps the best time to wander down La Rambla (Map p43, B4) is dawn on a crisp sunny day. The street cleaners have been through, the revellers are tucked up in bed and everything is strangely quiet.

By day and night, multitudes stream along this tree-lined pedestrian boulevard (flanked by two clogged traffic lanes), a stage for street performers (from flamenco dancers to fire-eaters and more human statues than you could knock over in one go), pickpockets, three-cups-and-a-ball tricksters and more. Rip-off pavement cafes, Australian pubs and newsstands bursting with porn add to the local colour, although Barcelonins are largely noticeable by their absence. As day turns to night, streetwalkers of all persuasions come out to play at the lower end of the boulevard, and many out-of-towners become more vocal as they revel into the wee hours.

La Rambla gets its name from a seasonal stream (*raml* in Arabic) that once ran here. By medieval times it was known as the Cagalell (from *caga,* meaning shit). This open-air sewer was filled in by the 18th century. La Rambla changes name five times along its 1.25km length, and if you can take your eyes off the human spectacle there is plenty to see, from Plaça de Catalunya to the Monument a Colom (p94).

You may well not even notice the modest Canaletes drinking fountain at the top end of the street, but this symbolic spot is the focus of celebrations for FC Barcelona football fans, who gather here whenever their side wins a famous victory.

Just north of Carrer del Carme, the Església de Betlem (p45) is one of the few baroque churches in Barcelona. Next up is the rococo

---

### ALL A-TWITTER

For more than 150 years, little birds and animals have been sold by 11 *ocellaires* (bird-keepers) on La Rambla. These stands have been fighting tooth and nail for several years for the right to stay, as their presence contravenes relatively new city rules on cruelty to animals. Watch this space.

Palau de la Virreina, while on the other side of La Rambla, Palau Moja is a rare example of the neoclassical. It houses the regional government bookshop and exhibition space. To the south, Plaça de la Boqueria is marked by a Miró pavement mosaic and the nearby La Boqueria market (p55).

Aside from the market, one thing that does attract Barcelona folks to La Rambla is the Gran Teatre del Liceu opera house (p46). Further on, you could pop into the Museu de Cera (p46), the wax museum.

# >3 MUSEU NACIONAL D'ART DE CATALUNYA

## ADMIRING CATALONIA'S ARTISTIC HERITAGE IN THE MUSEU NACIONAL D'ART DE CATALUNYA (MNAC)

As many Catalans will tell you, Catalonia is not Spain, but a nation with its own proud history. The collections inside the grand Palau Nacional (National Palace) are a worthy calling card for any country. The palace was raised from 1926 to 1929 as a magnificent, if temporary, pavilion for the 1929 World Exhibition.

There is nothing temporary about it today. The Museu Nacional d'Art de Catalunya is a one-stop immersion course on the world of (mostly) Catalan art, from medieval church frescoes to chairs designed by Gaudí. The highlight is the Romanesque art collection.

In the 1920s, art historians combed hundreds of churches dotting the northern Catalan countryside. Inside they uncovered unprecedented treasures: remains of bright Romanesque frescoes, some dating back to the 11th and 12th centuries. To save them from further decay, many were removed to Barcelona, and today they can be admired in the re-created interiors of those churches. The most striking frescoes are those of Mary and the Christ Child (Room 7), taken from the church of Santa Maria de Taüll in Catalonia's northwest, and the majestic depiction of Christ in Glory (Cristo Pantocrator, Room 5) from the nearby church of Sant Climent. Carvings and altar frontals complement the collection.

The Gothic art that follows is a broad-ranging mix, covering key Catalans such as Bernat Martorell and Jaume Huguet, and their contemporaries across Spain. Another highlight is the Thyssen-Bornemisza collection, with an eclectic range including works by Venetian Renaissance masters Veronese, Titian and Canaletto.

---

### ALWAYS LOOK ON THE BRIGHT SIDE

One Romanesque altar frontal (Room 10) depicts saints being boiled, having nails slammed into their heads and – always a crowd pleaser – being sawn in half from head to toe. In such images the saints always appear remarkably calm, a lesson to the brethren of the ultimate righteousness of those who die for the faith...but a hard act to follow!

Up on the next floor, Catalan artists of the realist, Modernista (Catalan Art Nouveau; including Ramón Casas and Santiago Rusiñol) and Noucentista (early-20th-century) movements are featured. Watch out for the comprehensive coin collection, which runs from Roman days to the present, and the fascinating photo gallery, with extensive black-and-white archives from the best of Catalan snappers. After such an intense dive into local culture, you'll be grateful for the museum's restaurant!

See p140 for more information.

# >4 MONTJUÏC

## WANDERING THE FRAGRANT GARDENS OF MONTJUÏC

Barcelona is one of the noisier cities in Europe, and there's no better antidote to the grinding decibel assault of traffic, road works, sirens and blaring music than a lazy day of strolling amid the beauty and serenity of soothing gardens, all the while gazing back on the urban madness below.

A trip to Montjuïc is already a must for its many fine museums, led by the Museu Nacional d'Art de Catalunya (MNAC; p140) and Fundació Joan Miró (p135; sculpture garden pictured right), but it's also worth coming here just for a wander.

Start at the Castell de Montjuïc (p135). Below its sandy walls, a walking path offers views over the wide blue sea. Follow it downhill (beside Carrer de Montjuïc) from the fort to arrive at the Jardins del Mirador, a good lookout point where a couple of snack bars await.

About 100m further on you reach the Jardins de Joan Brossa (p138). It's hard to believe there was once an amusement park in this delicately landscaped set of gardens bursting with Mediterranean flora, including cypresses, pines and the occasional palm.

Making your way west through the gardens, you exit at Carrer dels Tarongers. Across the road, the Jardins de Mossèn Cinto de Verdaguer (p138) are gentle, emerald, sloping gardens devoted to bulbs (tulips, dahlias, crocuses and more) and delicate water plants, such as lotus, water lilies and irises. There is no better spot in Barcelona for a snooze under a tree.

Away to the southwest is the Jardí Botànic (p138), a botanical garden that specialises in flora from places all over the world (from Australia to California) with a climate similar to that of the Mediterranean.

### GETTING AROUND MONTJUÏC

In addition to the PM public bus line, which covers much of Montjuïc, the hop-on, hop-off Bus Montjuïc Turístic (adult/child €3/2) operates two interlocking circuits daily from May to September (every 40 minutes from 10am to 9pm). The blue circuit starts at Plaça d'Espanya and the red circuit at Pla del Portal de la Pau, at the port end of La Rambla.

Down along Avinguda de Miramar, towards the port, the Jardins de Mossèn Costa i Llobera (p138) make for a final floral fling. The thundering traffic below robs this place of tranquillity, but the tropical and desert plants – including a veritable forest of cacti – are worth a look.

# >5 MODERNISME

## MARVELLING AT THE MANY ZANY MODERNISTA CREATIONS IN L'EIXAMPLE

If there is a part of town where you should always keep an eye skyward, l'Eixample is it. As you wander the grid of streets between Passeig de Sant Joan and Carrer de Muntaner, your eyes fall upon the splendid and whimsical facades of the countless buildings that Modernista architects raised in a few short decades around the turn of the 20th century. The closer you look at many of them, the more intriguing detail they reveal.

The star attractions line elegant Passeig de Gràcia. Among them are two of Gaudí's most eye-catching efforts: the undulating, stone-faced corner block of La Pedrera (p110); and the still crazier Casa Batlló (p105; pictured right), with its dragonlike roof. These can be visited, but it's best to arrive early as queues seem to be a permanent fixture.

On the same block as Casa Batlló are several other Modernista creations by rival architects. Of them all, Casa Amatller (p111), next door and done by Josep Puig i Cadafalch, stands out the most. It is a playful building, mixing pseudo-medieval with pseudo-Dutch elements. Take time to look at the facade and foyer – the most curious of sculpted figures jut out of walls and corners all over the place. A couple of houses down, Lluís Domènech i Montaner contributed the curvaceous Casa Lleó Morera (p111).

As you branch out, all sorts of marvels reveal themselves. Puig i Cadafalch was at his medieval jesting again with the gorgeous Palau del Baró Quadras (p112). Two blocks east, across Avinguda Diagonal, his Casa de les Punxes (p108) boasts fairytale turrets.

Some Modernista gems have taken on new roles. Casa Calvet (p121) is a high-flyers' restaurant, while Casa Fuster is now a luxury hotel.

Help is available for those who wish to track down these and other nuggets. See Modernisme Unpacked, p105, to get you started.

### WHAT'S IN A NAME?

Modernisme in Barcelona was part of a much wider phenomenon across Europe. The French called this new creative wave Art Nouveau (New Art), the Italians Liberty, the Austrians Sezession and the Germans Jugendstil (Youth Style).

# >6 MUSEU PICASSO

## PEERING AT PICASSO'S PRECOCIOUS GENIUS

Five hefty, stone, Gothic-baroque mansions in a row on medieval Carrer de Montcada are today occupied by Barcelona's Museu Picasso. The first three, Palau Aguilar (No 15), Palau del Baró de Castellet (No 17) and Palau Meca (No 19), all date from the 13th and 14th centuries and contain the permanent collection. The 18th-century Casa Mauri (No 21), built over medieval remains (even some Roman leftovers have been identified), and the 14th-century Palau Finestres (No 23) accommodate temporary exhibitions.

The permanent collection, with over 3500 pieces, is strongest on Picasso's earliest years, up until 1904. His talent is clear in adolescent works such as *Retrato de la Tía Pepa* (Portrait of Aunt Pepa) and *Ciència i Caritat* (Science and Charity), both completed in 1897. There are paintings from his early Paris sojourns and his first significant experimental stage, the Blue Period. His nocturnal, blue-tinted views of *Terrats de Barcelona* (Rooftops of Barcelona) and *El Foll* (The Madman) are spectral.

For those not expecting the usual round of Cubist masterpieces (noticeable by their absence), this is a rare voyage of discovery. If any proof was needed that Picasso had all the technical ability to turn out whatever he wanted, from giant canvases to whimsical self-portraits, you have it in abundance here.

See p79 for more information.

# >7 ESGLÉSIA DE SANTA MARIA DEL MAR

## MEDITATING ON TIMES PAST IN THE ESGLÉSIA DE SANTA MARIA DEL MAR

The grand Gothic church of Our Lady of the Sea was blessed in 1384. Standing before its sober entrance, flanked by two stout octagonal towers, you sense that this is quite unlike other European churches.

This is one of the purest examples of Catalan Gothic, generously broad and bereft of the baubles that characterise the Gothic temples of other climes. It was raised in record time, a mere 59 years, and is remarkable for its architectural harmony. Typically for the times, the church was raised around its Romanesque predecessor (itself on the site of an ancient Roman cemetery), which was progressively dismantled as work advanced.

As you admire this splendid feat of medieval construction, imagine the religious devotion of the city's porters, who spent a day each week carrying on their backs the stone required to build the church, trudging all the way from the royal quarries in Montjuïc. Their very blood is etched into the church's walls, and their memory lives on in reliefs of them on the main doors and stone carvings elsewhere in the church. Those who read Spanish should grab Ildefonso Falcones' *La Catedral del Mar* (Cathedral of the Sea), which tells this fascinating story.

See p75 for more information.

# >8 PARK GÜELL

## FALLING UNDER A SPELL IN PARK GÜELL

What a fine flop! What started in 1900 as the dream of a Barcelonin magnate, Eusebi Güell, for an English-style 'garden city' for the hoity-toity ended up as an enchanting public space. By 1914 Güell had given up on the original project, with only three of 60 planned blocks sold, but not before his favourite architect, Antoni Gaudí, had created 3km of sculpted paths, porticos, a plaza and two gatehouses.

At the main entrance on Carrer d'Olot, you'll feel you're entering Alice's Wonderland. You're greeted by two gingerbread houses of soft brown stone, topped by curvaceous, creamy-looking roofs decorated in *trencadís* (broken-up ceramics). The one on the right houses a display on Gaudí's building methods and the park's history.

Slip by the masses taking snaps of the ceramic-decorated lizard on the stairs, and head to the great pillared hall above, the Sala Hipóstila, which would have housed the garden city's market. Its roof is a grand viewing platform across the city, lined by the Banc de Trencadís, a delightful bench that snakes around its perimeter and is clad with candy-coloured ceramics.

See p130 for more information.

## >9 FC BARCELONA

### SITTING ON THE EDGE OF YOUR SEAT AT A BARÇA MATCH

For the sports-minded, little can match the glory and spectacle of a football match at FC Barcelona's Camp Nou stadium, one of the biggest and best in the world. The athletic genius of players in one of Europe's greatest clubs (founded in 1899) will have you sitting on the edge of your seat – along with 100,000 other spectators – when the stadium fills for big clashes, like the derby with arch-rivals Real Madrid.

The stadium is imposing, and on key match days people can be seen streaming towards it from all directions hours before kick-off. At night you may well notice a string of transsexual hookers in the streets around the stadium. This is their traditional patch, game or no game. By the ticket windows a squad of ticket scalpers operates more or less discreetly.

Although not the rowdiest supporters, local fans are ardent about their team and the atmosphere can be electric. For many, FC Barcelona (Barça to supporters) is the embodiment of the Catalan spirit.

See Follow the Balls, p148, for information on buying tickets.

HIGHLIGHTS

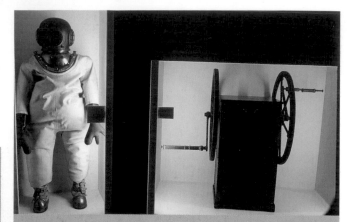

## >10 MUSEU MARÍTIM

**MUSING ON EPIC SEAFARING AT THE MUSEU MARÍTIM**

Climb aboard the life-sized replica of Don Juan of Austria's elaborately adorned 16th-century galley, and imagine life aboard this warship. Hundreds of men chained to the giant oars that drove this vessel at up to nine knots. The cracking of whips; the agony of this mix of slaves, prisoners and desperate volunteers. The sheer stench. These wretches ate, slept and went to the toilet where they sat. You could *smell* a medieval galley from miles away.

Don Juan's galley was launched here, at the Reials Drassanes (Royal Shipyards). The shipyards were completed in 1378 and are a superb example of civic Catalan Gothic architecture. As many as 30 galleys could be built beneath their lofty arches at any one time. The site has been a museum since the 1940s and is one of the most fascinating in the city. On display are vessels and models of all types, representing all epochs, from coastal fishing boats to giants of the steam age. There are also copies of intriguing medieval atlases and navigation charts, and dioramas re-creating life at sea and in port.

See p95 for more information.

## >11 EL RAVAL
### REVELLING IN EL RAVAL

Of the old town districts, El Raval is the grittiest and perhaps the sexiest. Long a slum and still edgy in parts, it is perfect for long nights crawling the bars.

Approach it from any angle. Just off the lower end of La Rambla is a classic little bar known for its dedication to French cabaret, Bar Pastis (p70). A short hop around the corner, luridly lit Kentucky (p72) was once a US Navy sailors' haunt in the depths of the then red-light district. Today it attracts local bohemians and out-of-towners. Nearby, Moog (p73) is a popular dance den. A block west, the Modernista London Bar (p72) has been drawing tipplers for a century, while Bar Marsella (p69; pictured above), on Carrer de Sant Pau, has been serving absinthe since the early 19th century.

# >12 MERCAT DE LA BOQUERIA

### TAKING A BITE OF MARKET LIFE IN LA BOQUERIA

This temple of temptation, known to all as La Boqueria, is one of Europe's greatest permanent produce fairs. Restaurant chefs, housewives and tourists all compete to get a look at the best of the day's goods.

Enter from La Rambla and you are plunged into a cornucopia of fruit, vegetables, sweets, nuts and more on the right. To the left you'll find cheeses, sausages, *jamón* (cured ham) and other cold meats. Maintain a direct course into the elliptical heart of the market and you'll arrive at the Illa del Peix (Fish Block), a series of stands creaking beneath the weight of tonnes of fresh, glistening seafood. Apart from classics such as flat grey *lenguado* (sole) and great chunks of *pez espada* (swordfish), you'll notice the burnt-red *gambes de Palamòs*, netted off the Costa Brava and among the tastiest (and dearest!) prawns on offer in Barcelona's restaurants.

At lunchtime, market workers and interlopers jostle for a stool at several bars in the market, among the better of which are Bar Pinotxo (p67) and Bar Central (p67).

See p55 for more information.

# >13 TIBIDABO

## CATCHING THE TIBIDABO TRAM AND SOME WILD RIDES

Come to the mountain. An old-style family outing, the trip to the city's highest peak, Tibidabo (512m), bursts with nostalgia. The panoramic vistas are themselves a fine reward; timeless amusement-park rides are a retro trip to fun parks of yore.

The Tramvia Blau (Blue Tram) clunks its way 1.3km up Avinguda del Tibidabo from Plaça de John F Kennedy to the amusement park's funicular station (one way/return €2.50/3.70). Virtually nothing has changed since the line opened in October 1901. From the polished timber seats, admire the fine mansions as you chug along. The single-wagon tram runs weekends and holidays (from 10am until at least 6pm) all year, and daily from late June to early September.

The funicular then whisks you to the top of the mountain, from where you can see the whole city. For still-better views (and often a chill wind), head for the roof of the Temple del Sagrat Cor (p151), or ride the lift to the top of the Torre de Collserola (p151).

The kids will no doubt drag you along to the Parc d'Atraccions (p150), Barcelona's old-style fun park.

# >14 GRÀCIA

## GRAPPLING WITH GRÀCIA'S LABYRINTH OF BUSY SQUARES AND NARROW STREETS

Gràcia bubbles with life. A separate town until 1897, its warren of straight, narrow streets and lanes opens up here and there onto a series of busy squares.

Check out the Modernista market at Plaça de la Llibertat (p130), completed in 1893, and the more down-to-earth produce market to the east, the Mercat de l'Abaceria Central (Map p129, C4). Take a look at Gaudí's early Modernista Casa Vicenç (p130) and then just wander. Swirl around with the locals in the bars and eateries, many of them gathered around a network of squares – the busiest are Plaça del Sol (C4), Plaça de la Virreina (C3) and Plaça de Rius i Taulet (C5). The last is fronted by the local town hall and dominated by the Torre del Rellotge (Clock Tower), long a symbol of republican agitation.

From Plaça de la Revolució de Setembre de 1868 (C4), pedestrian-only Carrer de Verdi runs northwest. It is lined by all sorts of tempting shops, eateries and bars, along with a good cinema (p133).

# >BARCELONA DIARY

Naturally inclined to enjoy themselves, Barcelonins put on a crammed calendar of events to suit every taste: from the fiery madness of the traditional summer solstice Nit del Foc and September's Festes de la Mercè, to theatre festivals, citywide jazz jams and Europe's top electronic music get-together. In summer (August especially), districts party in the streets in a series of local *festes* (festivals or parties) that involve bands, carousing and precious little sleep. For more on festivals, go to www.bcn.cat and click on Diary on the English homepage. For public holidays, see p190.

Turn on the sun – a colourful costume at Festes de la Mercè (p32)

# JANUARY

## Reis/Reyes

Christmas comes a couple of weeks later for Spanish children, as presents are traditionally distributed for the Epifanía (Epiphany) on 6 January. The evening before, children delight in the Cavalcada dels Reis Mags (Three Kings' Parade), with floats, music, and bucketloads of sweets chucked into the scrambling crowds.

## Festes dels Tres Tombs

A key part of the festival of Sant Antoni Abat (17 January) is this Feast of the Three Circuits, a parade of horse-drawn carts (St Anthony is the patron saint of

domestic animals) near the Mercat de Sant Antoni (Map p63, A4).

# FEBRUARY & MARCH

## Carnestoltes/Carnaval (Carnival)

Barcelona's carnival is colourful enough but the real fun happens in Sitges (see p140), where the gay community stages gaudy parades and party-goers let rip.

## Festival de Jazz

www.jazzterrassa.org
A major season of jazz concerts from mid-February to mid-March in the nearby city of Terrassa.

# MARCH & APRIL

## Divendres Sant/Viernes Santo (Good Friday)

Taste Andalucian Easter with processions from Església de Sant Agustí (Map p63, C4), featuring a float of the Virgin of the Macarena, robed members of religious fraternities and barefoot penitent women dragging crosses and chains.

## Dia de Sant Jordi

Catalonia celebrates St George on 23 April. Men give women a rose and women give men a book (it's also Dia del Llibre, Book Day).

---

### SUMMER STAGES & LATIN HEAT

Many theatres shut down for summer, but into the breach steps the **Festival del Grec** (www.barcelonafestival.com), with a program of theatre, dance and music from late June until well into August. Performances are held all over the city, not just at the open-air Teatre Grec amphitheatre on Montjuïc (Map pp136–7, E3), from which the festival takes its name. For Hispanic live music, **Barnasants** (www.barnasants.com) is hot. The city's live-music venues host a bevy of Catalan, Spanish and Latin American singer-songwriters for concerts from late January until mid-March.

Browse for a book on Dia de Sant Jordi (opposite)

# MAY & JUNE

## L'Ou Com Balla

The curious 'Dancing Egg' is an empty eggshell that bobs on top of the flower-festooned fountain in La Catedral's cloister to mark the feast of Corpus Christi (the Thursday after the eighth Sunday after Easter Sunday).

## Primavera Sound

www.primaverasound.com

For three days in late May and/or early June the Parc del Fòrum hosts international DJs

and musicians. A winter version, Primavera Club, takes place in early December.

## Sónar

www.sonar.es

Sónar is Barcelona's celebration of electronic music and Europe's biggest such event. See big names and experimental acts.

## Dia de Sant Joan (Feast of St John the Baptist)

The night before this feast day (24 June), people celebrate Berbena de Sant Joan (St John's Night), aka La Nit del Foc (Night of Fire), with drinking, dancing, bonfires and fireworks.

# AUGUST

## Festes de Sant Roc

For four days in mid-August, Plaça Nova (Map p43, B2) in the Barri Gòtic becomes the scene of parades, a *correfoc* (fire race), a market, traditional music and magic shows for kids.

## Festa Major de Gràcia

www.festamajordegracia.cat

Around 15 August, this knees-up in the Gràcia area features a competition for the best-decorated street. Enjoy feasting, bands and drinking.

## Festa Major de Sants

The district of Sants launches its own week-long version of decorated mayhem hard on Gràcia's heels, around 24 August.

## REACH FOR THE SKY

When there's a *festa major* (big festival) on in Catalonia, *colles* (teams) of *castellers* ('castlers', or human castle builders) gather to raise human 'castles' of at times astonishing height – up to 10 tiers. These usually involve levels of three to five people standing on each other's shoulders. A crowd of team mates forms a supporting scrum at the base. To complete the castle, a young (and light!) child called the *anxaneta* must reach the top and wave to the crowd, the signal to start whooping with abandon and to collapse (hopefully in orderly fashion) the castle. Watch out for *castellers* in Plaça de Sant Jaume (Map p43, C3) during the Festes de la Mercè.

# SEPTEMBER

## Festes de la Mercè

www.bcn.cat/merce

Barcelona's biggest party, with *castellers*, *sardanes* (folk dancing), *gegants* (giants), *capgrossos* (big heads), a *correfoc* and Barcelona Acció Musical (www.bcn.cat/bam in Catalan), a huge live-concert series.

# NOVEMBER

## Festival Internacional de Jazz de Barcelona

www.theproject.es

For most of the month, the big venues across town (from l'Auditori down) host a plethora of international jazz acts. At the same time, a more homespun jazz fest takes place in bars across the old city.

# >ITINERARIES

Steps leading up to the Sala Hipóstila at Park Güell (p22)

# ITINERARIES

Barcelona has enough sights to keep you exploring for months. Luckily, the city is compact, and most spots are easy to reach on foot or by Metro. When it's time for a break, there are plenty of tempting places to get a drink and a bite to eat.

## DAY ONE

A stroll along the rambunctious La Rambla (p12) is a must – duck into La Boqueria (p55) along the way. Once at the port, head back inland into the Barri Gòtic district. Make for Plaça de Sant Jaume and then La Catedral (p46). From here, cross Via Laietana, passing the colourful, reincarnated Mercat de Santa Caterina (p78), and veer southeast to reach the Museu Picasso (p79) and the Gothic Església de Santa Maria del Mar (p75). Take some time out for a wine at La Vinya del Senyor (p89) and check out the little fashion boutiques in the nearby side streets. Finish the day sampling seafood in one of the countless eateries in the backstreets of La Barceloneta (p95).

## DAY TWO

OK, you held off on day one, but your first stop on day two should be the magnificent Gaudí masterpiece, La Sagrada Família (p110). For a complete change of theme, head for Montjuïc. Star attractions on this hill include the Museu Nacional d'Art de Catalunya (p140), Fundació Joan Miró (p135), the Castell (p135) and strolls in the gardens (p16). Snack bars abound. Wander downhill into Poble Sec for evening gourmet snacks at Quimet i Quimet (p143), or a down-to-earth, roistering meal at La Tomaquera (p143) and a tipple at the unpredictable Tinta Roja (p144).

## DAY THREE

In summer you may well want some beach time. The better ones start with Platja de Nova Icària (p173), on the northeast side of Port Olímpic. Sea dogs should visit the Museu Marítim (p95). An excursion to Gaudí's marvellous Park Güell (p130) is also a good option, for its uniqueness and views. A meal in l'Eixample, perhaps at Cata 1.81 (p121), could be followed by dancing at Sutton The Club (p155).

**Top** Reflect on your purchases at mall-on-the-water Maremàgnum (p95) **Bottom** The fabulously plush Gran Teatre del Liceu (p46), Barcelona's eminent operatic stage

## A RAINY DAY

When it rains in Barcelona, it usually pours. Head first to the Museu d'Història de la Ciutat (p47), most of which is cosily underground and just a snap from the closest Metro stop! Palau del Lloctinent (p49) looks onto the same square. A quick dash gets you to the Museu Frederic Marès (p48). Virtually next door is the Casa de la Pia Almoina (p44) and then La Catedral (p46). For a sustenance stop, make a run for Cafè de l'Acadèmia (p56) for a great *menú del día* (set menu). When you're done with visiting the sights, head for Caelum (p50), a delightful den of delicacies that doubles as a cafe.

## MUSEUM MONDAYS

Many city sights shut on Mondays, but some buck the trend. Start with a bright art injection at the Museu d'Art Contemporani de Barcelona (p64), then wander the streets of El Raval to the Museu Marítim (p95). Now that you're all at sea, head for the waterfront in Port Vell. Ascend the Monument a Colom (p94), get a bite in the Maremàgnum shopping complex (p95) and proceed to l'Aquàrium (p91) for a shudder in the shark tunnel. Feeling energetic? Make for La Ribera and cross El Born to the Parc de la Ciutadella (p80), where you could finish the day at the Zoo de Barcelona (p81).

### FORWARD PLANNING

Opera and music lovers should think in advance. For a performance at the Gran Teatre del Liceu (p60), book on the internet as far ahead as possible. For the Palau de la Música Catalana (p89), a couple of weeks is usually enough.

Motor-racing fans can combine Formula One with partying in Barcelona each April. For dates contact the **Circuit de Catalunya** (www.circuitcat.com) racetrack. Book tickets online for this and many events at **ServiCaixa** (www.servicaixa.com). **FC Barcelona** ( ☎ 902 189900, from abroad 93 496 36 00; www.fcbarcelona.com) fans can check the schedule for upcoming games on the club's website, by phone or direct at the stadium. Major games tend to be booked solid weeks in advance.

For a fancy dinner, book a few days ahead at Saüc (p122) or, for a feast in a country-style mansion, at El Racó d'en Freixa (p152).

The day before you leave for Barcelona, check out the following for ideas on where to head at night: **Lecool** (www.lecool.com), **Agentes de la Noche** (www.agentesdelanoche.com in Spanish), **Barceloca** (www.barceloca.com), **BCN-Nightlife** (www.bcn-nightlife.com), **Barcelonarocks.com** (www.barcelonarocks.com), **Clubbingspain.com** (www.clubbingspain .com in Spanish) and **LaNetro.com** (http://barcelona.lanetro.com in Spanish).

CaixaForum (p135), an urban magnet for art-lovers

## FEELING SKINT

A busy day's sightseeing in Barcelona can be enjoyed while barely touching the wallet. You could start at Park Güell (p130), then continue the nature theme with a Metro and funicular ride to Montjuïc (p16) for a stroll around the gardens – the perfect spot for a packed picnic lunch, prepared with ingredients from La Boqueria (p55). Uphill, drink in the views over the Mediterranean from below the fortified walls of the Castell de Montjuïc (p135). It's free to wander into the Estadi Olímpic (p139). One of the few major museums with free entry is the delightful CaixaForum art gallery (p135), at the foot of the hill.

>NEIGHBOURHOODS

Shoppers ready to take on the delights of Passeig de Gràcia (p113)

# NEIGHBOURHOODS

Barcelona covers 100 sq km, a compact package jammed between the Mediterranean Sea and the Collserola mountain chain. The bulk of the sights are concentrated in the Ciutat Vella (Old City) and the adjoining l'Eixample district, with another concentration atop the Montjuïc hill.

The Ciutat Vella oozes 2000 years of history. Its core, the Barri Gòtic (Gothic Quarter), is bounded by the pedestrian spectacle of La Rambla and the thundering boulevard Via Laietana. In between soaring churches, medieval mansions and Roman reminders, its meandering lanes are laced with shops, bars and restaurants carved from centuries-old buildings.

Across La Rambla, El Raval is a slightly dodgier district that teems with bars and restaurants, along with the occasional streetwalker or junkie. La Ribera, northeast across Via Laietana, is home to Picasso's art, the city's greatest church and heaving nightlife around Passeig del Born.

Opening up at the seaward end of La Rambla, Port Vell (Old Port) is anything but aged, with a modern shopping and entertainment centre and a major aquarium. Nearby, La Barceloneta is a mix of working-class houses, sizzling fish restaurants and seemingly all of Europe's summertime youth draped along the beach. Beyond stretch more beaches, past the yachties' Port Olímpic and one-time industrial district of El Poblenou to the new coastal quarter of El Fòrum.

L'Eixample, repository of Modernista architecture, is divided into microzones. The gay scene, busy nightlife streets and endless sprinkling of restaurants demand exploration. Chic shopping congregates on and around Passeig de Gràcia and La Rambla de Catalunya. To the north, the slim fingers of Gràcia's lanes stretch into a labyrinth in what was once a separate town. Beyond lies Park Güell.

Southwest of l'Eixample, the streets of Poble Sec and Sants climb to the modest and verdant mountain of Montjuïc. Further north and west, stretching up to the city's highest point, Tibidabo (512m), are the wealthier districts that make up La Zona Alta.

# >BARRI GÒTIC & LA RAMBLA

Everyone walks La Rambla during a Barcelona stay. Visitors outnumber locals, but that just adds to the colour. In just a 1.25km strip you'll find bird stalls, flower stands, buskers, bars, historic shops, grand buildings, a pungent produce market, pickpockets, prostitutes, bored police and a veritable UN of paraders. Once a sewage ditch lined by medieval walls, La Rambla marks the southwest flank of what in the 20th century was dubbed the Barri Gòtic (Gothic Quarter).

This is where the Romans set up shop 2000 years ago. At its heart, the city and Catalan governments face each other on Plaça de Sant Jaume, where the forum was. Nearby are sprinkled Gothic mansions, the cathedral,

## BARRI GÒTIC & LA RAMBLA

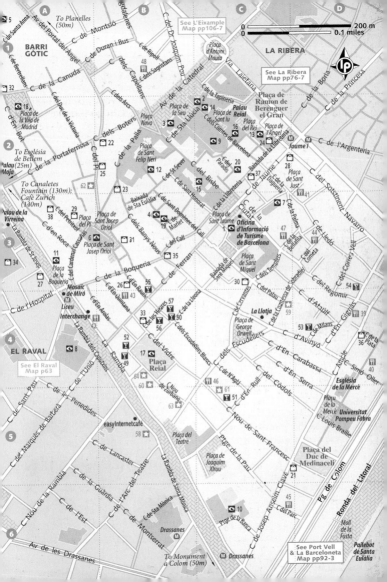

an underground slice of ancient Barcelona and leftover Roman walls. To the square's north and west, shoppers revel along Avinguda del Portal del Àngel and Carrer de la Boqueria. To the southeast, between crowded Carrer de Ferran and the port, narrow lanes are festooned with bars and eateries.

## ◉ SEE

The Barri Gòtic and La Rambla lend themselves to endless aimless wandering, but the principal sights are all clustered close by La Catedral in the heart of the ancient city.

### ◉ AJUNTAMENT
☎ 010; Plaça de Sant Jaume; 🕑 10am-1pm Sun; Ⓜ Jaume I
This town hall has been the seat of city power since the 14th century and has a Catalan Gothic side facade on Carrer de la Ciutat. Belying its blandly renovated, neoclassical front is a spectacular interior featuring a majestic staircase and the splendidly restored Saló de Cent (Chamber of the One Hundred).

### ◉ CASA DE LA PIA ALMOINA (MUSEU DIOCESÀ)
☎ 93 315 22 13; www.arqbcn.org in Catalan; Avinguda de la Catedral 4; adult/under 7yr/senior & student €6/free/3; 🕑 10am-2pm & 5-8pm Tue-Sat, 11am-2pm Sun; Ⓜ Jaume I
Barcelona's Roman walls ran across Plaça de la Seu into what subsequently became the Casa de la Pia Almoina. This charity operated from the 11th century,

but the present building dates back to the 15th century. Inside is the Museu Diocesà (Diocesan Museum), with a sparse collection of medieval religious art.

### ◉ CASA DE L'ARDIACA
Carrer de Santa Llúcia 1; admission free; 🕑 9am-9pm Mon-Fri, to 2pm Sat; Ⓜ Jaume I
This 16th-century house is home to the city's archives and has a supremely serene courtyard, renovated by Domènech i Montaner in 1902. You can get a good glimpse at some stout Roman walls inside the ground floor here.

### ◉ CENTRE D'INTERPRETACIÓ DEL CALL
☎ 93 256 21 22; www.museuhistoria.bcn.cat in Catalan & Spanish;

### ROMAN WALLS
Of course, the city's first architects of note were the Romans, who built a town here in the 1st century BC. Large relics of its 3rd- and 4th-century walls can still be seen in the Barri Gòtic, particularly at Plaça de Ramon de Berenguer el Gran (C2) and by the northern end of Carrer del Sotstinent Navarro (D2).

Placeta de Manuel Ribés/n; admission free; ⏰ 10am-2pm Wed-Fri, 11am-6pm Sat, 11am-3pm Sun & holidays; Ⓜ Liceu
The 14th-century house of the Jewish weaver Jucef Bonhiac now houses a small visitor's centre dedicated to the history of Barcelona's Jewish quarter, or Call. A few artefacts are on show.

### ⊙ ESGLÉSIA DE BETLEM
☎ 93 318 38 23; La Rambla dels Estudis; ⏰ 9am-2pm & 6-9pm; Ⓜ Liceu
The early-18th-century Church of Jerusalem was once considered the most splendid of Barcelona's few baroque offerings. Its exterior still makes a powerful impression, but arsonists destroyed much of the inside at the outset of the civil war in 1936. In the run-up to Christmas, check out the *pessebres* (nativity scenes).

### ⊙ ESGLÉSIA DE SANTA ANNA
☎ 93 301 35 76; Carrer de Santa Anna; ⏰ 9am-1pm & 6.30-8.30pm; Ⓜ Catalunya
Starting life as a Romanesque chapel in the 12th century, this tranquil house of worship is set on a square of its own and rarely visited. The deliciously silent and cool Gothic cloister encloses a leafy garden and fountain.

### ⊙ ESGLÉSIA DE SANTA MARIA DEL PI
☎ 93 318 47 43; Plaça del Pi; ⏰ 8.30am-1pm & 4.30-9pm Mon-Sat, 9am-2pm & 5-9pm Sun & holidays; Ⓜ Liceu
This striking church, built between 1322 and 1453, is a classic of Catalan Gothic, with an imposing facade, a wide interior and a single nave. The beautiful rose window

The world's largest rose window, above the entrance to the Gothic church Església de Santa Maria del Pi

above its entrance is thought to be the world's largest.

### ESGLÉSIA DE SANTS JUST I PASTOR
☎ 93 301 74 33; www.basilicasantjust
.cat in Catalan; Plaça de Sant Just 5;
🕙 11am-1pm & 5-9pm Wed-Sat, 11am-
2pm & 5-8pm Tue, 10am-1.30pm Sun;
Ⓜ Jaume I

This single-nave church was built in 1342 in Catalan Gothic style, with chapels on either side of the buttressing. It boasts some fine stained-glass windows. On Plaça de Sant Just, in front of the church, bubbles a water fountain dating from 1367. Gaudí was arrested here one day for not speaking Spanish to a copper.

### GRAN TEATRE DEL LICEU
☎ 93 485 99 00; www.liceubarcelona
.com; La Rambla dels Caputxins 51-59;
admission with/without guide €8.50/4;
🕙 guided tour 10am, unguided visits
11.30am, noon, 12.30pm & 1pm; Ⓜ Liceu

Built in 1847, burnt down in 1994 and resurrected five years later, this is Barcelona's grand operatic stage. Seating up to 2300, its horseshoe auditorium features restored 19th-century stalls combined with a hi-tech stage. The grand marble staircase and **Saló dels Miralls** (Hall of Mirrors) are among the few parts of the original building to survive the flames of 1994.

### LA CATEDRAL
☎ 93 342 82 60; Plaça de la Seu;
admission free, special visit €5; 🕙 8am-
12.45pm & 5.15-8pm daily, special visit
1-5pm Mon-Sat, 2-5pm Sun & holidays;
Ⓜ Jaume I

Barcelona's central place of worship was constructed in what was the northern half of the Roman town. The richly decorated main facade was added during the late 19th century (to a 15th-century design), while the rest of the cathedral was built between 1298 and 1460. Geese honk in the cloister, as they have since medieval times. In the middle of the central nave are the impressive 14th-century sculpted choir stalls (admission €2.20). The Sala Capitular (chapter house; admission €2) boasts a handful of religious paintings. Visit the roof and tower by lift (admission €2.20) from the Capella de les Animes del Purgatori near the northeast transept. In the morning or evening, entrance to the cathedral is free and you can visit any combination of the choir stalls, chapter house and roof. To visit all three, it costs less (and is less crowded) if you opt for the 'special visit'.

### MUSEU DE CERA
☎ 93 317 26 49; www.museocerabcn
.com; Passatge de la Banca 7; adult/under
5yr/senior & 5-11yr €7.50/free/4.50;
🕙 10am-10pm daily Jun-Sep, 10am-

1.30pm & 4-7.30pm Mon-Fri, 11am-2pm & 4.30-8.30pm Sat, Sun & holidays Oct-May; Ⓜ Drassanes

With a collection of 300 wax figures of familiar faces from around the world, this is just as creepy as any other wax museum. More disturbing than any display of twisted medieval torture are the figures of Prince Charles and Camilla.

### Ⓒ MUSEU DE L'ERÒTICA

☎ 93 318 98 65; www.erotica-museum .com; La Rambla de Sant Josep 96; adult/ senior & student €7.50/6.50; ⏱ 10am-midnight Jun-Sep, 11am-9pm Oct-May; Ⓜ Liceu

Falling somewhere between titillation, tawdriness and art, this private collection is devoted to sex through the ages. The decor is pseudo-seedy, and the diverse exhibits range from exquisite *Kama Sutra* illustrations and Mapplethorpe photos to early porn movies, S&M apparatus and a 2m wooden penis.

### Ⓒ MUSEU DEL CALÇAT

☎ 93 301 45 33; Plaça de Sant Felip Neri 5; admission €2.50; ⏱ 11am-2pm Tue-Sun; Ⓜ Liceu

This little museum of shoes is an unexpected treat: there are dainty ones, famous ones, weird ones, Roman ones, silk ones, seamless ones, baby ones and one gigantic one made for the Monument a Colom (p94).

### Ⓒ MUSEU D'HISTÒRIA DE LA CIUTAT

☎ 93 256 21 00; www.museuhistoria .bcn.cat in Catalan & Spanish; Carrer del Veguer; adult/under 7yr/senior & student €6/free/4 (incl Museu-Monestir de Pedralbes & Park Güell Centre d'Interpretació), from 4pm 1st Sat of month free; ⏱ 10am-8pm Tue-Sat, 10am-3pm Sun Apr-Sep, 10am-2pm & 4-7pm Tue-Sat, 10am-3pm Sun Oct-Mar; Ⓜ Jaume I

The entrance to this museum is through the 16th-century mansion Casa Padellàs, which was shifted here, stone by stone, in the 1930s to make way for the bustling ramrod artery of Via Laietana. Digging the foundations one day, what should labourers stub their shovels on but the ancient Roman city of Barcino. Descend into the remnants of the Roman town and stroll along glass ramps above 2000-year-old streets. Walk past the old public laundries, where pots were left outside for passersby to pee in – urine was used as a disinfectant in Roman laundries! Explore public baths and drainage systems. Peer into storage areas for wine (Catalan wine was plentiful and rough) and *garum* (a whiffy fish sauce popular throughout the Roman empire). After Barcino, you emerge into the buildings of the Palau Reial, the former royal palace, where you can admire the broad arches of the Saló del Tinell, a 14th-century banquet hall.

###  MUSEU FREDERIC MARÈS

☎ 93 256 35 00; www.museumares
.bcn.es; Plaça de Sant lu 5-6; adult/under
16yr/senior & student €4.20/free/2.40,
Wed afternoons & 1st Sun of month free;
⏱ 10am-7pm Tue-Sat, to 3pm Sun &
holidays; Ⓜ Jaume I

Within these centuries-old walls resides a mind-boggling collection of art, medieval Spanish sculpture and everyday items of 19th-century daily life. It was amassed by Frederic Marès i Deulovol (1893–1991),

sculptor, traveller and hoarder extraordinaire. Among the most eye-catching pieces is a reconstructed Romanesque doorway with four arches, taken from a 13th-century country church in the Aragonese province of Huesca. Have a snack in the shady courtyard cafe.

### PALAU DE LA GENERALITAT

Plaça de Sant Jaume; admission free;
⏱ guided tours 10am-1pm 2nd & 4th
Sun of month plus 23 Apr, 11 Sep & 24
Sep; Ⓜ Jaume I

This seat of Catalan government was adapted from several Gothic

Statues of baby Jesus (middle statue by Francisco Salzillo), Museu Frederic Marès

mansions in what had been the Jewish ghetto (known as the Call) in the early 15th century, and was extended over time. The original Gothic facade on Carrer del Bisbe features a relief of St George, completed by Pere Joan in 1418. If you wander by in the evening, squint up through the windows into the Saló de Sant Jordi (Hall of St George) and you will get some idea of the sumptuousness of the interior. Bring ID for a tour.

### ☪ PALAU DEL LLOCTINENT

Carrer dels Comtes de Barcelona; admission free; ☪ 10am-7pm; Ⓜ Jaume I

Built in the 1550s, this palace was the residence of the *lloctinent* (Spanish viceroy) of Catalonia. It boasts a fine wooden ceiling and pleasing courtyard, and is home to the Arxiu de la Corona d'Aragó, a unique archive documenting the history of the kingdom prior to unification under Fernando and Isabel. Exhibitions, usually related in some way to the archives, are also staged.

### ☪ PLAÇA REIAL

Ⓜ Liceu

This pretty 19th-century square, with neoclassical facades, palm trees and numerous noisy restaurants and bars, was created on the site of a convent. The elegant lamp posts were Gaudí's first commission in the big smoke.

### ☪ ROMAN CEMETERY

Plaça de la Vila de Madrid; Ⓜ Catalunya

On a quiet square that once lay on a road leading out of Roman Barcino, this site features a series of intact Roman tombs lined up on the spot where they were found.

### ☪ SINAGOGA MAJOR

☎ 93 317 07 90; www.calldebarcelona .org; Carrer de Marlet 5; admission €2; ☪ 11am-6pm Mon-Sat, to 3pm Sun; Ⓜ Liceu

The remains of what is mooted by some to be the Jewish ghetto's main medieval synagogue (not all archaeologists agree with the claim) were accidentally discovered in the early 2000s. In the two rooms, now again a working temple, you can see remnants of

### STROLL ALONG CARRER DE LA DAGUERIA

If you're striding away from Plaça de Sant Jaume towards Via Laletana, stop to make a right down the delightful medieval lane of Carrer de la Dagueria (C2). In less than 100m you'll encounter a cheese shop, a ceramics vendor, a women's bookshop and a handful of bars and places to eat. The street ends in Plaça de Sant Just, walled off to one side by the Església de Sants Just i Pastor (p46) and graced by a scattering of outdoor tables for a drink or snack.

Roman-era walls and some tanners' wells.

### ⊙ TEMPLE ROMÀ D'AUGUSTI
**Carrer del Paradis 10; ⌚ 10am-2pm Mon-Sat; Ⓜ Jaume I**
It's unremarkable from the outside, but this courtyard houses four Corinthian columns of Barcelona's main Roman temple, built in the 1st century in the name of Caesar Augustus. Opening hours can be unreliable.

## 🛍 SHOP
The teensy lanes of the Barri Gòtic are jammed with shops. Carrer d'Avinyó is something of a youthful fashion strip, while sky-high-rent Avinguda del Portal del Àngel hosts a mix of all sorts. Exploration will throw up some eye-catching curiosities.

### ⬜ ANTINOUS *Books*
**☎ 93 301 90 70; www.antinouslibros .com in Spanish; Carrer de Josep Anselm Clavé 6; ⌚ 11am-2pm & 5-8.30pm Mon-Fri, noon-2pm & 5-8.30pm Sat; Ⓜ Drassanes**
An extensive bookshop with his-and-hers gay literature, Antinous is also a centre of Barcelona's gay culture. Out the back is a relaxed cafe, which doubles as an exhibition space and stage for book presentations.

### ⬜ ART MONTFALCON
*Gifts, Art*
**☎ 93 301 13 25; www.montfalcon.com; Carrer dels Boters 4; Ⓜ Liceu**
Beneath the overarching vaults of this Gothic cavern is spread an incredible range of gift ideas and art. The most appealing are the prints of local and universal inspiration. Thrown in are original works by local artists, framed and ready to go, and a whole range of Barcelona memorabilia, from ceramics to arty T-shirts. International shipment service is available.

### ⬜ CAELUM *Food & Drink*
**☎ 93 302 69 93; Carrer de la Palla 8; ⌚ 10.30am-8pm Tue-Thu & Sun, 11.30am-11pm Fri & Sat, 5-8pm Mon; Ⓜ Liceu**
From all corners of the country arrive the carefully prepared sweets and other goods that have been the pride of Spanish convents

down the centuries. Tempting traditional items such as sticky marzipan (made in closed-order convents) and olive oil with thyme find their way into this specialist store. Head downstairs to the cavernous cafe, once a medieval Jewish bathhouse. You can also take a seat at a huddle of tables upstairs.

### CERERIA SUBIRÀ *Candles*
☎ 93 315 26 06; Baixada de la Llibreteria 7; 🕑 9am-1.30pm & 4-7.30pm Mon-Fri, 9am-1.30pm Sat; Ⓜ Jaume I
Even if you're not interested in flickering flames, you'll be impressed by the ornate decor here. Nobody can hold a candle to these people in terms of longevity – the Subirà name in wax and wicks has been in demand since 1761,

### BOUTIQUES GALORE ALONG CARRER D'AVINYÓ
Not so many years back, this was a lugubrious lane. What a transformation! Commencing at Carrer Ample (D4) and working its way to Carrer de Ferran (B3), Carrer d'Avinyó is festooned with small fashion boutiques, such as Urbana (No 39), Perlimpinpin (No 46), Àngel Gimeno (No 25), Cirkus (No 24), Storm (No 20), Sita Murt (No 18) and many others. The startling, narrow, gaudy neoclassical Llotja, about halfway along, is a design and art school.

although it's only been at this address since late in the 19th century.

### DRAP *Dolls*
☎ 93 318 14 87; www.miniaturasdrap.com; Carrer del Pi 14; Ⓜ Liceu
This busy shop brings out the giddy little girl in all of us – which generally comes as a surprise to blokes – as it's packed to the rafters with everything relating to dolls and their well-being, from miniature jars of jam to intricate handmade mansions.

### EL INGENIO *Masks, Costumes*
☎ 93 317 71 38; www.el-ingenio.com; Carrer d'En Rauric 6; Ⓜ Liceu
Liven up your party with El Ingenio's bewildering range of tricks, fancy dress, masks and other accessories. Pick up a stick-on Salvador Dalí moustache, or ride out on a unicycle in a devil's outfit. The shop's been doing this since the mid-19th century!

### ESCRIBÀ *Food & Drink*
☎ 93 301 60 27; www.escriba.es; La Rambla de Sant Josep 83; 🕑 8.30am-9pm; Ⓜ Liceu
Chocolates, dainty pastries and mouth-watering cakes can be lapped up behind the Modernista mosaic facade here or taken away for quiet, private and guilt-ridden consumption. This Barcelona

**NUGGETY CHRISTMAS NOSH**

When Christmas comes, specialist pastry stores fill with *turrón*, the traditional holiday temptation (and tooth-rotter). Essentially nougat, it comes in all sorts of varieties, although at the base is a sticky almond concoction. Softer blocks are known as *turrón de Valencia* and a harder version as *turrón de Gijón*. You can find it year-round, but for the best wait until Christmas and check out stores like **Planelles** ( ☎ 93 317 34 39; www.planellesdonat.com; Avinguda del Portal del Àngel 27; ⏰ 10am-9pm Mon-Sat, 4-9pm Sun & holidays; Ⓜ Catalunya). It also does great ice creams and *orxata*, the summer tiger-nut drink from Valencia. The Planelles family first started selling Christmas nougat in the 1850s.

favourite is owned by the Escribà family, a name synonymous with sinfully good sweet things.

🏠 **FC BOTIGA**
*Football Paraphernalia*
☎ 93 269 15 32; Carrer de Jaume I 18;
⏰ 10am-9pm; Ⓜ Jaume I
Need a Messi football jersey, a blue-and-burgundy ball, or any other soccer paraphernalia pertaining to what many locals consider the greatest team in the world? This is a convenient spot, and one of a growing number of such outlets (six at the time of writing) around town, to load up without traipsing out to the stadium.

🏠 **GANIVETERIA ROCA**
*Homeware*
☎ 93 302 12 41; www.ganiveteriaroca
.es; Plaça del Pi 3; Ⓜ Liceu
If it needs to be cut, clipped, snipped, trimmed, shorn, shaved or cropped, you'll find the perfect in-

strument at this classic gentlemen's shop, going strong since 1911. You'll also find wine paraphernalia (who'd have thought there were so many kinds of bottle-openers and corkscrews?!) and kitchen accessories.

🏠 **GOTHAM** *Antiques*
☎ 93 412 46 47; www.gotham-bcn.com;
Carrer de Cervantes 7; Ⓜ Jaume I
This great retro shop specialises in furniture and decor items (originals and reproductions) from the 1930s, '50s, '60s and '70s. Mosaic-covered tables, strangely curving seats that remind you of *Lost in Space,* and lurid lamps are just the tip of the often kitsch iceberg.

🏠 **LA CONDONERIA**
*Condoms, Erotica*
☎ 93 302 77 21; www.lacondoneria
.com; Plaça de Sant Josep Oriol 3;
Ⓜ Liceu
Spaniards call them *consoladores,* a much nicer word than dildos. If

Step back in time and avail yourself of the medicinal herbs at L'Herboristeria del Rei

you've left yours at home, this is a cheerful spot to find a replacement. While you're at it, stock up on orange-scented lube and perhaps a packet of lurid green ribbed condoms.

### ☐ LE BOUDOIR *Lingerie, Erotica*
☎ 93 302 52 81; www.leboudoir.net; **Carrer de la Canuda 21;** Ⓜ **Catalunya**
It's not just about stylish, matt-black vibrators and penis rings. In this sensually sexy shop you'll find anything from vibrating G-strings to night masks, incense to whips, and candy bras to books on the arts of love and seduction.

### ☐ L'HERBORISTERIA DEL REI
*Herbs*
☎ 93 318 05 12; www.herboristeriadel rei.com; **Carrer del Vidre 1;** ⏱ **10am-8pm Tue-Sat;** Ⓜ **Liceu**
This soothing shop is framed by a grand balcony and lined with the tiny drawers of herbal specimens that have kept it in business since 1823. You'll find anything from teas to tinctures here. The shop took its name when it became court herbalist to Queen Isabel II. Tom Tykwer shot scenes of *Perfume: The Story of a Murderer* here.

### Pilar Sánchez
*Fishmonger at Mercat de la Boqueria (opposite)*

**What's your name?** They call me Pilarín. **What time do you get working at the market?** We start here at 8am and go through to 1pm, although sometimes we do different shifts, pretty much every day. It's a family business and I've always worked here. **I thought maybe earlier...** Oof, that's the last thing I need! **Where does all the fish come from?** Some is local, some comes from Galicia (northwest Spain). It depends on the catch. **Where do you get the fish from? Do you deal directly with fishermen?** No, we buy it at the central market (Mercabarna) and some at the beaches. **Have things changed much down the years?** No, it's always been much the same, but nowadays there are a lot of tourists, too. **But you manage to work anyway?** People still eat, right?

GAMBA
FRESCA
37€

LANGOS
1C

## MARKET SQUARES
Make the most of Barcelona's many markets:
> **Plaça Nova** (Map p43, B2) Antiques and bric-a-brac on Thursday.
> **Plaça de Sant Josep Oriol** (Map p43, B3) Arts and crafts on Saturday and Sunday.
> **Plaça del Pi** (Map p43, A3) Handmade food products Friday to Sunday every fortnight.
> **Plaça Reial** (Map p43, B4) Stamps and coins on Sunday morning.
> **Mercat de Sant Antoni** (Map p63, A4) Old maps, stamps, books and cards on Sunday morning.

### 🏠 MERCAT DE LA BOQUERIA
*Market*
☎ 93 318 25 84; La Rambla de Sant Josep 91; ⏱ 8am-8.30pm Mon-Sat; Ⓜ Liceu
One of Europe's best and most famous markets (see p26), this bustling produce hall is laden with atmosphere, colour and all the ingredients that make Spanish cuisine a favourite at the kitchen table.

### 🏠 OBACH *Millinery*
☎ 93 318 40 94; Carrer del Call 2; Ⓜ Liceu
If the hat ever makes a comeback, the Obach family of milliners, in the heart of what was once the Jewish quarter, stands to make a killing. Since 1924 it has been providing gentlemen with apparel for their scones.

### 🏠 PAPABUBBLE *Food & Drink*
☎ 93 268 86 25; www.papabubble.com; Carrer Ample 28; ⏱ 10am-2pm & 4-8.30pm Tue-Fri, 10am-8.30pm Sat, 11am-7.30pm Sun, closed Aug; Ⓜ Drassanes
They really make the boiled sweets here in front of your eyes!

Sample the wares and try to resist walking away without a big jar of humbugs and other multicoloured wonders, or a house speciality – a life-sized candy phallus.

### 🏠 RAG SHOP *Fashion*
☎ 93 319 78 61; Carrer de la Llibreteria 14; Ⓜ Jaume I
Skunkfunk, a ballsy Basque Country brand that is taking the urban women's prêt-à-porter world by storm, leads the way in this casual fashion boutique. Mix and match light summer dresses and easy-going tops.

### 🏠 SALA PARÉS *Art*
☎ 93 318 70 20; www.salapares.com; Carrer del Petritxol 5; ⏱ 4-8pm Mon, 10.30am-2pm & 4-8pm Tue-Fri, 10.30am-2pm & 4.30-8.30pm Sat, 11.30am-2pm Sun; Ⓜ Liceu
In business since 1877, this private gallery has maintained its position as one of the city's leading purveyors of Catalan art, both old and contemporary. Picasso exhibited

here and the gallery continues to concentrate on seeking out home-grown talent.

# 🍴 EAT

The Barri Gòtic's twisting streets and lanes throw up all sorts of surprises, so keep your eyes peeled at every turn. From centuries-old Catalan classics to avant-garde hideaways and some of the city's best Japanese nosh, you never know what you might turn up in this medieval labyrinth.

### 🍴 AGUT Catalan €€

☎ 93 315 17 09; Carrer d'En Gignàs 16; 🕑 lunch & dinner Tue-Sat, lunch Sun, closed Aug; Ⓜ Jaume I; ✕

This friendly family-run restaurant appeals to a sedate crowd that digs its traditional and robust Catalan fare. The *suquet de rap* (monkfish stew) is finger-licking good, but there are succulent sirloin steaks for greater sustenance. You might start with *bouillabaisse con cigalitas de playa* (fish stew with little seawater crayfish).

---

### MENÚ DEL DÍA

Most restaurants offer a set lunch menu (*menú del día*, or meal of the day), which usually consists of three courses and a drink. The meals typically cost around €8 to €12, a good deal less than ordering à la carte.

---

### 🍴 BAR CELTA Tapas €

☎ 93 315 00 06; Carrer de la Mercè 16; 🕑 noon-midnight; Ⓜ Drassanes

The stormy Atlantic in Spain's northwest yields seafood goodies that wind up in bars like this as tapas. *Pulpo a la gallega* (boiled octopus in a slightly spicy oil mix) is one. Accompany it with a shallow ceramic cup of crisp Ribeiro white wine.

### 🍴 CAFÈ DE L'ACADÈMIA
Catalan €€

☎ 93 319 82 53; Carrer de Lledó 1; 🕑 lunch & dinner Mon-Fri; Ⓜ Jaume I; ✕

An old favourite with hungry, hard-working public servants in the nearby Ajuntament, this cafe never fails to satisfy their demands. The key to its success is a solid grounding in well-prepared local cuisine with the occasional inventive twist. The atmosphere hums good-naturedly at lunchtime but is rather more subdued and romantic in the evening. Try for a seat in the square.

### 🍴 CAFÈ DE L'ÒPERA Cafe €

☎ 93 302 41 80; La Rambla dels Caputxins 74; 🕑 9am-3am; Ⓜ Liceu; ✕

This busy cafe is the most atmospheric on La Rambla, having stood the test of time. Bohemians and their buddies mingle with tourists beneath art-deco images of opera heroines etched into mirrors.

### 🍴 CAFÈ ZURICH *Cafe* €
☎ 93 317 91 53; Carrer de Pelai 39;
🕑 8am-11pm Sun-Fri, 10am-midnight
Sat; Ⓜ Catalunya; ✕

The original 1920s Cafè Zurich was
one of the city's landmark meeting
places, but it was torn down in 1997
to make way for the department
store now on this corner. The cafe's
pseudoclassic replacement may
not have the same charm, but the
outside tables are perfectly placed
for watching the world go by.

### 🍴 CAN CULLERETES
*Catalan* €€
☎ 93 317 30 22; Carrer d'En Quintana 5;
🕑 lunch & dinner Tue-Sat, lunch Sun;
Ⓜ Liceu; ✕

Founded in 1786, Barcelona's oldest restaurant is still going strong,
with tourists and locals flocking to
its rambling interior, old-fashioned
tiled decor, and enormous help-
ings of traditional Catalan food.
Service with a snarl is compensat-
ed for by the timeless setting.

### 🍴 COMETACINC
*Fusion* €€
☎ 93 310 15 58; www.cometacinc.com;
Carrer del Cometa 5; 🕑 dinner Wed-
Mon; Ⓜ Jaume I; ✕

This atmospheric medieval den
turns out an ever-changing menu
of items that transgress all culinary
boundaries. Salads come in unexpected mixes, or you could opt for

a pseudo-Thai dish. The candlelit
tables over two floors add a touch
of romantic intimacy.

### 🍴 EL PARAGUAYO
*South American* €€
☎ 93 302 14 41; Carrer del Parc
1; 🕑 lunch & dinner Tue-Sun;
Ⓜ Drassanes

Forget about Catalan refinements,
teasing tapas or avant-garde pre-
tensions. Here the word is meat –
great juicy slabs of the stuff. Tuck
into all sorts of tasty cuts of beef,
pork and other flesh in this little
Latin American oasis.

### 🍴 LOS CARACOLES *Catalan* €€
☎ 93 302 31 85; Carrer dels Escudellers
14; 🕑 lunch & dinner; Ⓜ Drassanes; ✕

The Barri Gòtic's most pictur-
esque restaurant is with little
doubt this 19th-century tavern.
It's famous for spit-roasted
chickens and – as the name suggests – snails (from the town of
Vic, north of Barcelona). Largely
frequented by tourists in the
evenings, it is still a highly atmospheric place (and the snails are
not bad at all!).

### 🍴 PLA *Fusion* €€
☎ 93 412 65 52; www.pla-repla.com;
Carrer de la Bellafila 5; 🕑 dinner;
Ⓜ Jaume I; ✕

The chicest choice in the Gothic
quarter, Pla has black-and-white

NEIGHBOURHOODS

BARRI GÒTIC & LA RAMBLA

menus featuring photographs of staff in action. It mainly serves innovative modern Mediterranean dishes with an Asian twist, beneath a splendid medieval stone arch.

### 🍴 SHUNKA Japanese €€

☎ 93 412 49 91; Carrer dels Sagristans 5; 🕐 lunch & dinner Tue-Sun; Ⓜ Jaume I

Shunka is a cut above Barcelona's Asian average. The presence of Japanese punters is reassuring, and the open-plan kitchen also inspires confidence – you can keep an eye on what they're doing with your tempura and sashimi.

# 🍸 DRINK

Plaça Reial is surrounded by bars and dance clubs. From there, the spider web of lanes unravelling roughly to the east and south also have plenty of offerings.

### 🍸 BARCELONA PIPA CLUB
Bar

☎ 93 302 47 32; www.bpipaclub.com; Plaça Reial 3; 🕐 11pm-4am Sun-Thu, to 5am Fri & Sat; Ⓜ Liceu

Ring the buzzer at one of the most intriguing bars in the city. It's a genuine pipe-smokers' club by day, and transforms into a dim, laid-back and incurably cool bar at night. Generally it's for members only until 11pm.

### 🍸 CLUB ROSA Bar

Carrer d'En Rauric 23; 🕐 8pm-2.30am Sun-Thu, to 3am Fri & Sat; Ⓜ Liceu

A Gothic bar for the Gothic quarter, with a couple of baroque touches (such as the heavy gilt-framed mirror). An Addams Family collection of dark paintings, dim lamps, dripping candles, chilled music and even cooler cocktails create a deliciously conspiratorial atmosphere.

### 🍸 CLUB SOUL Bar-Club

☎ 93 302 70 26; Carrer Nou de Sant Francesc 7; 🕐 10pm-2.30am Mon-Thu, 10pm-3am Fri & Sat, 8pm-2.30am Sun; Ⓜ Drassanes

This backstreet treasure (still known to many as Dot Light Club) has a cosy bar at the front for an intimate chat (on the single sofa), and an equally diminutive, congenial dance floor out the back. Each night the DJs change the musical theme, ranging from deep funk to Latin grooves.

### 🍸 GLACIAR Bar

☎ 93 302 11 63; Plaça Reial 3; 🕐 4pm-2.30am; Ⓜ Liceu

With its marble bar and timber seating inside, and aluminium tables and chairs outside beneath the porch, Glaciar is an age-old classic for warm-up tipples and watching the free street theatre of Plaça Reial.

## MANCHESTER *Bar*

☎ 663 071748; www.manchesterbar
.com; Carrer de Milans 5; ⏱ 7pm-2.30am
Sun-Thu, to 3am Fri & Sat; Ⓜ Jaume I or
Drassanes

Feeling nostalgic for the sounds of
Manchester? This is the place to fill
up on the Smiths, the Buzzcocks,
the Stone Roses and other bands
associated with the city. Inside,
red is the predominant shade
and cocktails the principal tipple.
It has a sister joint in the El Raval
neighbourhood.

## MILK BAR & BISTRO *Bar*

☎ 93 268 09 22; Carrer d'En Gignàs 21;
⏱ 11am-4pm (brunch) & 6.30pm-3am;
Ⓜ Jaume I

Smiling bar staff, 1920s wallpaper,
comfortable lounges and gently
wafting chill-out music all conspire
to create an inviting ambience for
a languorous tipple or three. The
cocktails at this establishment are
inventive, light meals are available
and the brunch is a formidable
hangover cure.

## SCHILLING *Bar*

☎ 93 317 67 87; Carrer de Ferran 23;
⏱ 10am-2.30am Mon-Thu, 10am-3am
Fri & Sat, noon-2am Sun; Ⓜ Liceu

No, it's not new, nor is it hidden
away anywhere, and increasingly
it's filled with out-of-towners rather than locals. But this gay-friendly
favourite remains a great place
to sip on a glass of wine or two
before heading out into a more ad-
venturous night. Grab a tiny round
marble table if you can and ignore
the somewhat frosty service.

Start your evening sipping a drink at Schilling

NEIGHBOURHOODS

BARRI GÒTIC & LA RAMBLA

### ▼ SINATRA *Bar*
☎ 93 412 52 79; Carrer de les Heures 4-10; ⏲ 9pm-2.30am; Ⓜ Liceu
A block off Plaça Reial, Sinatra is no tepid piano bar, but a raucous and somehow pleasing place to take a Desperados beer while listening to '80s tracks. Cowhide seating and a mirror ball complete the slightly retro feel. You'll be hard pushed to find too many Spaniards in here, though.

### ▼ SUGAR *Bar*
Carrer d'En Rauric 21; ⏲ 8pm-2.30am Sun-Thu, to 3am Fri & Sat; Ⓜ Liceu
This funky little cave is proof that you can go a long way with very little. Throw a few cushions (it could do with more) around the entrance cubby hole and benches; add a bar, DJ, red lighting and cocktails; and stir. A fun place to hang out before clubbing.

## ⭐ PLAY
From a night at the opera to long nights of jazz or a little flouncing flamenco, several night-time options present themselves.

### ⭐ CLUB FELLINI *Club*
☎ 687 969825; www.clubfellini.com; La Rambla dels Caputxins 27; admission €15; ⏲ midnight-5am Mon-Sat May-Sep, midnight-5am Mon & Thu-Sat Oct-Apr; Ⓜ Drassanes

Sitting between peep shows and a striptease hall, this long-time club comes into its own on slow Monday nights. Pop along for rock 'n' roll and indie rock at the Nasty Mondays session. The club has three spaces: the Bad Room for house, electro and punk; the Red Room for pop and rock; and the Mirror Room, a bigger, more chilled space.

### ⭐ GRAN TEATRE DEL LICEU *Opera*
☎ 93 485 99 00; www.liceubarcelona.com; La Rambla dels Caputxins 51-59; admission €7.50-150; ⏲ box office 2-8.30pm Mon-Fri, 1hr before show Sat & Sun; Ⓜ Liceu
Some good can come of disasters. Fire in 1994 destroyed this old dame of opera, but the reconstruction has left Barcelona with one of the most technologically advanced theatres in the world. It remains a fabulously plush setting for your favourite aria.

### ⭐ HARLEM JAZZ CLUB *Live Music*
☎ 93 310 07 55; Carrer de la Comtessa de Sobradiel 8; admission up to €10; ⏲ 8pm-4am Tue-Thu & Sun, to 5am Fri & Sat; Ⓜ Jaume I or Drassanes
Deep in the Barri Gòtic, this smoky dive is the first stop for jazz aficionados. Sessions include traditional and contemporary jazz along with creative fusions from around the

world. There's usually more than one cosy session an evening.

### ⭐ JAMBOREE *Live Music*
☎ 93 319 17 89; www.masimas.com/jamboree; Plaça Reial 17; admission up to €10; ⏱ 9.30pm-6am; Ⓜ Liceu
Jamboree has long brought joy to the jivers of Barcelona, with headline jazz and blues acts of the calibre of Chet Baker and Ella Fitzgerald. The tradition lives on. Gigs usually start at 11pm and proceed until about 2am, at which point punters convert themselves into clubbers heaving to hip hop and flailing to funk.

### ⭐ LA MACARENA *Club*
Carrer Nou de Sant Francesc 5; admission up to €5; ⏱ 11pm-4am Sun-Thu, to 6am Fri & Sat; Ⓜ Drassanes
A very dark dance space, this is the sort of intimate spot where it is possible to sit at the bar, meet people around you and then have a bit of a grind to the DJs' electro and house offerings, all within a couple of square metres.

### ⭐ MALDÀ ARTS FORUM
*Cinema*
☎ 93 481 37 04; Carrer del Pi 5; admission up to €8; Ⓜ Liceu
Should a sudden desire for a movie strike while you're in the

heart of the Barri Gòtic, this curious little cinema is worth a look. It often has an interesting original-version movie or two on offer.

### ⭐ NEW YORK
*Club*
☎ 93 318 87 30; Carrer dels Escudellers 5; admission €10; ⏱ midnight-6am Thu-Sun; Ⓜ Drassanes
Until the mid-1990s, this street was lined with dingy bars of ill-repute. New York was one of them, but it's been reborn as a popular old-town club space attracting dancers from 18 to 30. Friday night is best, with anything from reggae to Latin rhythms.

### ⭐ SALA TARANTOS
*Flamenco*
☎ 93 319 17 89; www.masimas.com/tarantos; Plaça Reial 17; admission from €6; ⏱ 10pm-6am Mon-Sat; Ⓜ Liceu
Locals and tourists get hot and steamy with flamenco, Latin and salsa sessions here. A one-hour *tablao* (flamenco performance) takes place three times a night most nights. On an altogether un-flamenco note, Wednesday night (from 11.30pm) is WTF Vocal Jams night, where daring souls try their luck singing in a live show.

# >EL RAVAL

El Raval (and especially its lower half, known as the Barri Xinès, or Chinese Quarter, an odd name that means 'red-light district') was long an old-city slum and all-round louche quarter. To some extent it still is.

It is doubtless the most colourful of the three Ciutat Vella (Old City) districts, home to a strong migrant community (mostly Pakistanis and North Africans) and still a haunt for down-and-outs, prostitutes and the occasional drug dealer. At the same time, the opening of the Macba contemporary art gallery, CCCB cultural centre, and enormous philosophy and history faculties of the Universitat de Barcelona have injected new life. New housing has gone up around La Rambla del Raval, where a luxury hotel is also nearing completion.

The massive arrival of local students and tourists has further transformed the district. Classic bars and restaurants have been joined by all manner of sparkling new places, some snooty, some grungy. Awaiting discovery are a Romanesque church and one of Gaudí's early commissions.

Petty theft is common around here (and indeed in much of the old city), so remain sharp and don't wander around with any more valuables than you strictly need.

## EL RAVAL

### ◉ SEE
Antic Hospital de la
  Santa Creu...................**1** B4
Centre de Cultura
  Contemporània de
  Barcelona ...................**2** B3
Església de Sant Pau
  del Camp ....................**3** B5
Museu d'Art
  Contemporani de
  Barcelona ...................**4** B3
Palau Güell ...................**5** C4

### ◓ SHOP
Castelló...........................**6** B2
El Indio ...........................**7** C3

Etnomusic......................**8** B3
La Portorriqueña...........**9** B3
Lefties ..........................**10** A2

### 🍴 EAT
Bar Central ...................**11** C4
Bar Kasparo .................**12** B3
Bar Pinotxo .................**13** C3
Biblioteca ....................**14** C4
Biocenter......................**15** B3
Casa Leopoldo .............**16** B4
Elisabets.......................**17** B3
Fidel..............................**18** A3
Granja Viader ...............**19** C3
L'Havana.......................**20** A3
Restaurant El Cafetí .....**21** B4
Sesamo.........................**22** A4

### ▼ DRINK
Bar Marsella .................**23** C5
Bar Muy Buenas ...........**24** B4
Bar Pastís.....................**25** D5
Betty Ford ...................**26** A3
Boadas...........................**27** C2
Bodega La Penúltima....**28** A4
Casa Almirall................**29** A3
Kentucky.......................**30** D5
Kiosco La Cazalla..........**31** D4
La Confitería.................**32** B5
London Bar....................**33** C5
Marmalade....................**34** B4

### ★ PLAY
Moog ............................35 D5

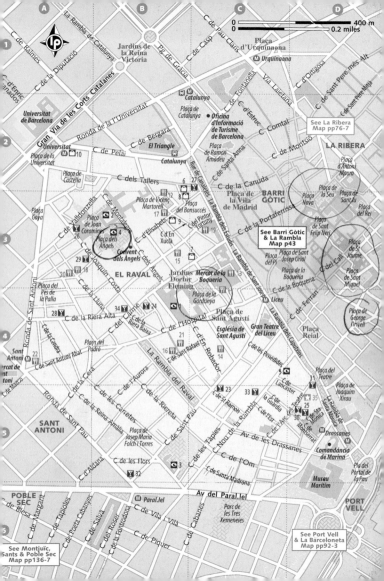

# 👁 SEE

## 👁 ANTIC HOSPITAL DE LA SANTA CREU

☎ 93 270 23 00; Carrer de l'Hospital 56; admission free; 🕑 library 9am-8pm Mon-Fri, to 2pm Sat; Ⓜ Liceu

Gaudí died at this 15th-century hospital, which now houses Catalonia's national library, an arts school and the Institut d'Estudis Catalans (Institute for Catalan Studies). You can freely visit the most impressive part, the grand reading rooms beneath broad Gothic stone arches, where you can also see temporary displays of anything from old records to medieval monastic hymnals. Otherwise, it is possible to join a tour on 23 April (Dia de Sant Jordi) and one day late in September (the date changes), when the entire building throws itself open for guided visits. It has a delightful, if somewhat dilapidated, colonnaded courtyard with a chirpy cafe. The **chapel** ( ☎ 93 442 71 71; www .bcn.cat/virreinaexposicions; 🕑 noon-2pm & 4-8pm Tue-Sat, 11am-2pm Sun & holidays) is used for temporary exhibitions.

### FAT CAT

*Gat*, the tubby tabby in La Rambla del Raval, is the work of Colombian artist Fernando Botero and was unveiled in 1992. The statue's biggest headache is the vandals who occasionally break off his whiskers!

## 👁 CENTRE DE CULTURA CONTEMPORÀNIA DE BARCELONA (CCCB)

☎ 93 306 41 00; www.cccb.org; Carrer de Montalegre 5; for 2 exhibitions adult/under 16yr/senior & student €6/free/4.40, for 1 only €4.40/free/3.30; 🕑 11am-8pm Tue, Wed & Fri-Sun, to 10pm Thu; Ⓜ Universitat

Loved by locals, this dynamic, multi-use cultural centre occupies the shell of an 18th-century hospice, with sgraffiti decoration in the main courtyard. It hosts a constantly changing program of exhibitions on urban design, 20th-century arts, architecture and the city itself.

## 👁 ESGLÉSIA DE SANT PAU DEL CAMP

☎ 93 441 00 01; Carrer de Sant Pau 101; 🕑 cloister 10am-2pm & 5-7pm Tue-Fri, 10am-2pm Sat; Ⓜ Paral.lel

Barcelona's oldest church, St Paul in the Fields was founded by monks in the 9th century. Although the squat, rural-looking building shows its age, it has some wonderful Visigothic sculptural decoration on its doorway and a fine Romanesque cloister.

## 👁 MUSEU D'ART CONTEMPORANI DE BARCELONA (MACBA)

☎ 93 412 08 10; www.macba.es; Plaça dels Àngels 1; adult/concession €7.50/6, Wed €3.50; 🕑 11am-8pm Mon & Wed,

Get a bright art injection in the polished Museu d'Art Contemporani de Barcelona (Macba)

11am-midnight Thu & Fri, 10am-8pm Sat, 10am-3pm Sun & holidays late Jun-late Sep, 11am-7.30pm Mon & Wed-Fri, 10am-8pm Sat, 10am-3pm Sun & holidays late Sep-late Jun; M Universitat

The ever-expanding contemporary art collection of the Macba starts in the Gothic chapel of the Convent dels Àngels and continues in the main gleaming-white building across the square. It shines as a stage for the best of Catalan, Spanish and international contemporary art. What's on show is in constant, restless flux, although in the chapel you are more likely to see established names such as Alexander Calder and Antoni Tàpies.

## PALAU GÜELL

☎ 93 317 39 74; www.palauguell.cat; Carrer Nou de la Rambla 3-5; admission free; ☾ 10am-2.30pm Tue-Sat; M Drassanes or Liceu

With this commission for wealthy patron Eusebi Güell, Antoni Gaudí first showed what he was capable of. Sombre compared with his later whims, it is still a characteristic riot of styles (Gothic, Islamic, art nouveau) and materials. Following the civil war, the police tortured political prisoners in the basement. Up two floors you reach the main hall and its annexes. The hall is a parabolic pyramid – each wall is an arch, stretching up three floors and coming together to form a dome. The roof is a Gaudi-an carnival of ceramic colour and fanciful design in the chimney pots. It was only partly open at the time of writing.

# 🛍 SHOP

For CDs, Carrer dels Tallers is the place to go – it is lined with music stores. Carrer de la Riera Baixa is where you'll find army cast-offs and second-hand clothes, while the area south of the Macba is peppered with little art galleries and the like.

### 🛍 CASTELLÓ *Music*
☎ 93 318 20 41; www.discoscastello.es; **Carrer dels Tallers 7;** Ⓜ **Catalunya**
This family-run chain has been tickling the ears of Catalans since 1935, and has five stores in El Raval. Each specialises in a different genre so, between them, you're bound to hit the right chord. Aside from the main branch, try Carrer dels Tallers 3 for classical music; No 9 for alternative, hip-hop and other contemporary sounds; and No 79, another general store.

### 🛍 EL INDIO *Fabrics*
☎ 93 317 54 42; **Carrer del Carme 24;** Ⓜ **Liceu**
You may well not want to buy anything at 'The Indian', but just walking into this fabric store with

> ## PRELOVED ON CARRER DE LA RIERA BAIXA
> Looking for fashion bargains, perfect for passing unnoticed in this 'hood? In little more than 100m, starting on Carrer de l'Hospital (B4) and finishing on Carrer del Carme (B4), you'll find the best part of a dozen clothes shops, mostly second-hand. For some variety, a couple of second-hand record stores and the nicely restored Bar Resolis, perfect for a mid-shopping refreshment, are thrown into the bargain.

the Modernista shopfront is like stepping a century back in time.

### 🛍 ETNOMUSIC *Music*
☎ 93 301 18 84; www.etnomusic.com; **Carrer del Bonsuccés 6;** 🕑 5-8pm Mon, 11am-2pm & 5-8pm Tue-Sat; Ⓜ **Catalunya**
From flamenco to samba and a whole lot in between, this is your best bet for music from around the globe. It's a higgledy-piggledy little place but the friendly staff will bend over backwards in search of the CD you're after.

### 🛍 LA PORTORRIQUEÑA
*Food & Drink*
☎ 93 317 34 38; **Carrer d'En Xuclà 25;** 🕑 9am-2pm & 5-8pm Mon-Fri, 9am-2pm Sat; Ⓜ **Catalunya**
Forget Starbucks: this is coffee. Beans from around the world are

freshly ground before your eyes in the combination of your choice. This place has been in the coffee business here since 1902. It also purveys all sorts of chocolate goodies.

### 🏠 LEFTIES *Fashion*
☎ 93 317 50 70; Carrer de Pelai 2; Ⓜ Universitat

Lefties (ie leftovers) is a top spot for men's, women's and kids' fashions from the previous year at silly prices. Fill your wardrobe with perfectly good, middle-of-the-road threads and your bank manager will be none the wiser.

# 🍴 EAT

Some of the city's classic eateries are scattered about the streets of El Raval. Otherwise, you might want to crowd in for lunch at one of several options in the Mercat de la Boqueria (p55). Some very reasonable options line Carrer de Sant Pau.

### 🍴 BAR CENTRAL *Catalan* €€
☎ 93 301 10 98; Mercat de la Boqueria; ⌚ lunch Mon-Sat; Ⓜ Liceu

Towards the back of Barcelona's emblematic produce market is one of the best of several market eateries for a hearty lunch. Marketeers, local workers and the occasional curious tourist jostle for a stool. Go for the grilled fish of

the day or perhaps some chunky *mandonguilles* (meatballs).

### 🍴 BAR KASPARO
*Mediterranean* €€
☎ 93 302 20 72; Plaça de Vicenç Martorell 4; ⌚ 9am-10pm; Ⓜ Catalunya

Pull up a stainless-steel pew for terrace dining beneath vaults at this friendly Australian-run place, on the corner of a pleasant square with swings for the kids. It does a sturdy line in snacks, mixed salads, filled rolls and hot dishes that change daily.

### 🍴 BAR PINOTXO *Catalan* €€
☎ 93 317 17 31; Mercat de la Boqueria; ⌚ 6am-5pm Mon-Sat, closed Aug; Ⓜ Liceu

Of the half-dozen or so tapas bars and informal eateries within the market, this one near the La Rambla entrance is about the most popular. Roll up to the bar and enjoy the people-watching as you munch on tapas assembled from the products on sale in the stalls around you.

### 🍴 BIBLIOTECA
*Mediterranean* €€
☎ 93 412 62 21; Carrer de la Junta del Comerç 28; ⌚ dinner Mon-Fri, lunch & dinner Sat, closed 2 weeks in Aug; Ⓜ Liceu

In a long ground-floor setting, with bare brick walls and stylishly simple white decor, the 'Library' presents a changing menu of mixed dishes. Taking Navarran and Mediterranean cuisine as a base, the chef produces such items as *cérvol estofat amb pasta fullada i puré* (a steaming venison pie).

### 🍴 BIOCENTER *Vegetarian*　€
☎ 93 301 45 83; Carrer del Pintor Fortuny 25; 🕑 1-5pm Mon & Tue, 1-5pm & 8-11.15pm Wed-Sat; Ⓜ Catalunya; ✗ Ⓥ ♿

You share your table with whomever at this large and friendly veggie restaurant, serving a great assortment of salads, casseroles and seasonal vegetables cooked using various techniques from around the world. Head past the coffee bar through the dining area, with its warm exposed brickwork and dark timber tables, to the kitchen at the back to order your *menú del día* (set menu; €11.45). Augment it with as much salad as you can stand at the open salad buffet.

### 🍴 CASA LEOPOLDO
*Catalan*　€€€
☎ 93 441 30 14; www.casaleopoldo .com; Carrer de Sant Rafael 24; 🕑 lunch & dinner Tue-Sat, lunch Sun, closed Easter & Aug; Ⓜ Liceu; ✗

Several rambling dining areas in this 1929 classic, all sporting magnificent tiled walls and exposed timber-beam ceilings, make this

a fine option for lovers of local tradition. The seafood menu is extensive and the wine list is strong on the local product.

### 🍴 ELISABETS *Catalan*　€€
☎ 93 317 58 26; Carrer d'Elisabets 2-4; 🕑 lunch Mon-Thu & Sat, lunch & dinner Fri, closed Aug; Ⓜ Catalunya; ♿

Thank God places like this haven't been swept away by the rising tide of gleaming, trendy, could-be-anywhere, avant-garde locales. What about good old food that hits the comfort spot? The walls are lined with old radio sets, and the lunch menu varies daily. Try the throaty, gamey flavour of the *ragú de jabalí* (wild-boar stew).

### 🍴 FIDEL *Bocadillos*　€
☎ 93 317 71 04; Carrer de Ferlandina 24; 🕑 1pm-1am Mon-Thu, 6.30pm-2.30am Fri-Sun; Ⓜ Universitat; Ⓥ

For some of the tastiest *bocadillos* (filled rolls) in town, Fidel is unbeatable. This hideaway, with marble-top tables, funky background music and dozens of tempting *bocadillos* (including some vegetarian options with cheese), is a long-standing fave with Barcelonins.

### 🍴 GRANJA VIADER
*Dairy Bar*　€
☎ 93 318 34 86; Carrer d'En Xuclà 4; 🕑 9am-1.45pm & 5-8.45pm Tue-Sat, 5-8.45pm Mon; Ⓜ Catalunya; ♿

The fifth generation of the same family runs this atmospheric milk bar and cafe, set up in 1873 as the first to bring farm freshness to the city. They invented *cacaolat*, the chocolate-and-skimmed-milk drink now popular all over Spain, and continue to be innovative purveyors of all things milky. Try a cup of homemade hot chocolate and whipped cream (ask for a *suís*).

### ☎ L'HAVANA *Catalan* €€
☎ 93 302 21 06; Carrer del Lleó 1; ⏰ lunch & dinner Tue-Sat, lunch Sun; Ⓜ Sant Antoni

Time stands still in this back-alley, family-run, Catalan classic. The front dining area, with frosted-glass windows, some Modernista design touches and spaciously spread tables, is a touch more severe than the better-lit rear area. Dig into *calamars farcits* (stuffed calamari) and follow with homemade *crema catalana* (a Catalan version of crème brûlée).

### ☎ RESTAURANT EL CAFETÍ
*Catalan* €€
☎ 93 329 24 19; Passatge de Bernardí; ⏰ lunch & dinner Tue-Sat, lunch Sun; Ⓜ Liceu; ✂

Down a narrow arcade off Carrer de Sant Rafael, this cosy upstairs eatery is crammed with antique furniture and offers traditional local cooking, with one or two un-

orthodox variations. Paella and a dozen other rice dishes dominate.

### ☎ SESAMO
*Vegetarian* €
☎ 93 441 64 11; www.sesamo-bcn.com; Carrer de Sant Antoni Abat 52; ⏰ lunch & dinner Mon & Wed-Sat, dinner Sun; Ⓜ Sant Antoni; ✂ Ⓥ

For 'food without beasts', this relaxed corner eatery attracts all sorts. Drop by for juices and pastries at breakfast, a three-course set lunch (€9) or dinner. Wafting electronica is almost soothing and nice touches include the home-baked bread and cakes.

# ☒ DRINK

Students hang out in the many bars on and just off Carrer de Joaquín Costa. Otherwise, a smattering of watering holes, many with a century or so of history, are scattered across the district, with a particular concentration between Carrer de Sant Pau and Carrer de l'Arc del Teatre.

### ☒ BAR MARSELLA *Bar*
Carrer de Sant Pau 65; ⏰ 10pm-2am Mon-Thu, to 3am Fri & Sat; Ⓜ Liceu

This place looks like it hasn't had a lick of paint since it opened in 1820. Assorted chandeliers, tiles and mirrors decorate its one rambunctious room, which on weekends is packed to its rickety rafters with a cheerful mishmash of shady characters, slumming uptowners and Erasmus students, who all stop by to try the absinthe.

### Y BAR MUY BUENAS Bar
☎ 93 442 50 53; Carrer del Carme 63; ⏲ 7.30am-2.30am; Ⓜ Liceu

What started life as a late-19th-century milk bar is now lacking the milk. The Modernista decor and relaxed company make this a great spot for a quiet mojito, perhaps some live music and Middle Eastern nibbles.

### Y BAR PASTÍS Bar
☎ 93 318 79 80; Carrer de Santa Mònica 4; ⏲ 7.30pm-2am Sun-Fri, to 3am Sat; Ⓜ Drassanes

Although French cabaret chanson dominates, you might just as easily find yourself confronted by a little bossa nova or tango, depending on when you wander into this pleasingly cluttered shoebox of a bar, in business since WWII.

### Y BETTY FORD Bar
☎ 93 304 13 68; Carrer de Joaquín Costa 56; ⏲ 6pm-2am Mon-Thu, to 3am Fri & Sat; Ⓜ Universitat

This enticing corner bar is one of several good stops along the

### RUNNING THE GAUNTLET ON CARRER DE SANT RAMON

A trip to the legendary Bar Marsella (p69) can also involve a brief walk on the wild side. Along its flank runs Carrer de Sant Ramon, though there's nothing very saintly about this street. In two short blocks you'll see an international brigade of streetwalkers, their pimps, drug dealers and occasionally just a bunch of older locals animatedly discussing football in the middle of the road.

student-jammed run of Carrer de Joaquín Costa. It does nice cocktails and the place fills with an even mix of locals and foreigners, generally not much over 30 and with an abundance of tats and piercings.

### Y BOADAS Cocktail Bar
☎ 93 318 88 26; Carrer dels Tallers 1; ⏲ noon-2am Mon-Thu, to 3am Fri & Sat; Ⓜ Catalunya

One of the city's oldest cocktail bars, Boadas is famed for its daiquiris. The bow-tied waiters have been serving up unique drinkable creations since Miguel Boadas opened the bar in 1933. They specialise in short, intense drinks. The house speciality is the sweetish Boadas, with rum, Dubonnet and Curaçao.

## ⅄ Maria Dolores Boadas
*Co-owner of Boadas (opposite), one of Barcelona's oldest cocktail bars*

**When were you were born?** I was born at home just two years after Papa (Miguel Boadas) opened this bar in 1933. **How did it all begin?** My father was born in Havana (Cuba) and was the first barman at La Floridita (owned by a cousin and one of Hemingway's favourites). My father was Cuban… and so am I! He came to Barcelona in the 1920s. **You also met your husband here…** In 1957 I came downstairs one day and saw a man (José Luis Maruenda, now co-owner of the bar) smoking a pipe. He soon came back to ask my father permission to take me out. 'Take care of her,' Papa said. 'I've only got one (daughter).' **You never thought about going elsewhere?** I'm a Boadas… I've always been here. Here behind the bar, I'm me! (Maria Dolores still whips up a mean cocktail.)

## ▼ BODEGA LA PENÚLTIMA *Bar*

**Carrer de la Riera Alta 40;** ⏰ **7pm-2am Tue-Thu, to 3am Fri & Sat, to 1am Sun;** Ⓜ **Sant Antoni**

There is a baroque semidarkness about this dark timber and sunset-yellow place, which gives off airs of an old-time wine bar. In Spanish lore, one never drinks *la última* (the last one) as it is bad luck. Rather, it is always the 'second-last' round. A mixed group crowds into the lumpy lounges around uneven tables at the back, or huddles at the bar for endless second-last rounds of wine, beer or cocktails.

## ▼ CASA ALMIRALL *Bar*

☎ **93 318 99 17; Carrer de Joaquín Costa 33;** ⏰ **7pm-2.30am;** Ⓜ **Universitat**

People have been boozing here since 1860, which makes it the oldest continuously functioning bar in Barcelona. Delightfully dishevelled, it still has its original Modernista bar.

## ▼ KENTUCKY *Bar*

☎ **93 318 28 78; Carrer de l'Arc del Teatre 11;** ⏰ **10pm-3am Tue-Sat;** Ⓜ **Drassanes**

Once a popular hang-out for US Navy personnel when the boys were in town, this narrow exercise in Americana kitsch is a smoke-filled, surreal drinking dive, almost always packed to the rafters. Po-

lice laxity permitting, it often stays surreptitiously open until 5am.

## ▼ LA CONFITERÍA *Bar*

☎ **93 443 04 58; Carrer de Sant Pau 128;** ⏰ **11am-2am;** Ⓜ **Paral.lel**

A confectioner's shop until the 1980s, this place has barely changed its look in its conversion into a laid-back bar. The original cabinets are now lined with booze instead of bonbons. Perfect for coffee and paper during the day, it is jammed with local revellers at night.

## ▼ LONDON BAR *Bar*

☎ **93 318 52 61; Carrer Nou de la Rambla 34;** ⏰ **7.30pm-3am;** Ⓜ **Drassanes**

In the heart of the once-notorious Barri Xinès district, this bar was founded in 1910 as a hang-out for circus hands, and drew the likes

### THE HOLE IN THE WALL

The **Kiosco La Cazalla** (Carrer de l'Arc del Teatre; ⏰ 10am-9pm Mon-Wed, to 2.30am Thu-Sat; Ⓜ Drassanes), little more than a square metre of bar punched into the wall, serves thirsty passers-by beer, wine and, most importantly, the morello-cherry-based firewater known as *cazalla*. This little-known Andalucian beverage, often served with a few raisins floating in it, is an acquired taste (some Italians claim it is similar to sambuca). A shot of 50-proof *cazalla* costs €1.50.

The Modernista London Bar has been drawing tipplers for a century

of Picasso and Miró in search of local colour. With the occasional band playing out the back and a wonderful mix of local customers and travellers, it remains a classic.

### MARMALADE *Bar*

**☎ 93 442 39 66; www.marmaladebarcelona.com; Carrer de la Riera Alta 4-6; 7pm-3am; M Sant Antoni**

From the street you can see the golden hues of the back-lit bar way down the end of a long, lounge-lined passageway. To the left of the bar, by a bare brick wall, is a pool table, popular but somehow out of place in this chic, ill-lit chill den (with attached restaurant). Happy hour (cocktails €4) is from 7pm to 9pm.

## PLAY

### MOOG *Club*

**☎ 93 301 72 82; www.masimas.com/moog; Carrer de l'Arc del Teatre 3; admission €8; 11.30pm 5am; M Drassanes**

Moog (named after the synthesiser) is reliable for techno and electronica, and always packed with a young, enthusiastic crowd. Bigger in stature than in size, it attracts lots of big-name DJs. Upstairs specialises in indie retro pop numbers and is better for conversationalists.

# >LA RIBERA

An integral part of the Barri Gòtic until it was split off by Via Laietana in the early 1900s, La Ribera was medieval Barcelona's economic power-house. You'll know you're in what was once one of the wealthiest streets in medieval Barcelona, Carrer de Montcada, when you see the queues outside the centuries-old mansions that constitute the Museu Picasso. In the 12th century, when Barcelona emerged as one of the main Mediterra-nean trading hubs, Carrer de Montcada was laid out to connect the then waterfront with one of the main roads from the city to Rome.

In medieval times, activity was especially great around Passeig del Born, a short leafy boulevard behind Barcelona's mightiest Gothic church, Santa Maria del Mar. But the area declined as trading routes closed, and until the early 1990s it was dotted with a handful of sad old bars. Today, the timeless lanes are crammed with restaurants, bars and boutiques. To the northeast stretches the green lung of Parc de la Ciutadella.

## LA RIBERA

Please see over for map

# SEE

Modernista jewels, Picasso's museum and the city's greatest Gothic church head up the list of sights in this busy slice of old Barcelona. There are plenty of curiosities besides, from a chocolate museum to the city zoo and a marvellous modern market.

## ARC DE TRIOMF
**Passeig de Lluís Companys; M Arc de Triomf**

This curious triumphal gate, with its Islamic-style brickwork, was the ceremonial entrance to the 1888 Universal Exhibition. What triumph it commemorates isn't clear – probably just getting the thing built more or less on time.

## ESGLÉSIA DE SANTA MARIA DEL MAR
**☎ 93 319 05 16; Plaça de Santa Maria del Mar; ⏰ 9am-1.30pm & 4.30-8pm; M Jaume I**

Detail of the imposing Arc de Triomf

Barcelona's most powerful and beguiling Catalan Gothic temple (see p21) stands serenely amid the swirling crowds that daily invade the El Born area. The church was built in just 59 years and is the city's most graceful. The main body is made up of a central nave and two flanking

## CHURCHES BURNING

Conscription of Catalans for Spain's imperialist war in Morocco lit the fuse of anarchism among disaffected workers in Barcelona in 1909. Protests spilled over into full-scale rioting against the establishment, and 70 churches, including the Església de Santa Maria del Mar (above), were torched during what came to be known as the Setmana Tràgica (Tragic Week). The anarchists attracted popular support, and when the civil war broke out in 1936 they again vented their spleens on the churches, gutting everything from La Sagrada Família (p110) to the Església de Santa Maria del Pi (p45).

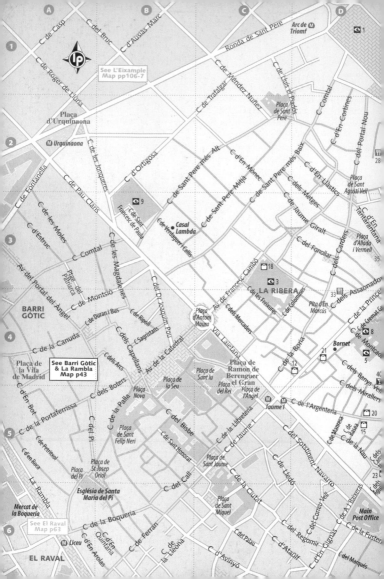

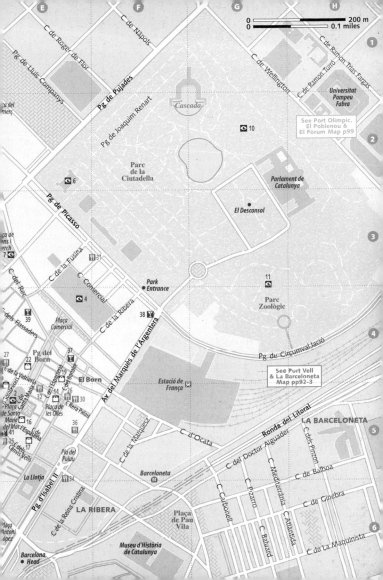

## E

C de Roger de Flor
C de Nàpols
Pg de Lluís Companys
a del
C de Pujades
Pg de Joaquim Renart

## F

## G

C de Wellington

## H

C de Ramon Trias Fargas
C de Ramon Turró
Universitat Pompeu Fabra

200 m
0.1 miles

1

*Cascada*

10

2

See Port Olímpic, El Poblenou & El Fòrum Map p99

Parc de la Ciutadella

6

Parlament de Catalunya

3

El Desconsol

a de
ns i
rch
7

Pg de Picasso

C del Rec

C de la Fusina
31

Comercial

4

Park Entrance

C de la Ribera

38

11

Parc Zoològic

4

dels Flassaders
39

Plaça Comercial

Pg de Circumval·lació

See Port Vell & La Barceloneta Map pp92–3

27
Pg del Born
22
37

C de la Vidriera
19

El Born

C del Comerç

Av del Marquès de l'Argentera

Estació de França

Ronda del Litoral

LA BARCELONETA

5

2
32
Plaça de Santa Maria
16
del Mar
41
25
dels
Canvis Vells
17

44
Plaça de les Olles
30
36

C de la Marquesa

C d'Ocata

C del Doctor Aiguader

C dels Pinzón

C de Balboa

La Llotja
34

Pg d'Isabel II

Pla del Palau

Barceloneta

C de la Maquinista

6

Plaça Antoni López

LA RIBERA

C de la Reina Cristina

Plaça de Pau Vila

Museu d'Història de Catalunya

Barcelona Head

aisles separated by slender octagonal pillars, creating an enormous
sense of lateral space. Opposite its
southern flank, an eternal flame
burns over a sunken square. This
was El Fossar de les Moreres (the
Mulberry Cemetery), where Catalan
resistance fighters were buried after
the siege of Barcelona ended in
defeat in September 1714.

### MERCAT DE SANTA CATERINA

www.mercatsantacaterina.net; Avinguda de Francesc Cambó 16; 🕙 8am-
2pm Mon, to 3.30pm Tue, Wed & Sat, to
8.30pm Thu & Fri; Ⓜ Jaume I
This 21st-century produce market,
with an undulating, polychrome-
tiled roof, is a great place to shop
for fresh produce and gourmet
products, as well as to stop for
lunch. Local architect Enric Miralles
designed it on the site of its 19th-
century predecessor, which itself
replaced a medieval Dominican
monastery. Some excavated
remnants of the monastery are on
show.

### MERCAT DEL BORN

Plaça Comercial; Ⓜ Barceloneta
The long-silent 19th-century
Mercat del Born is destined to
become a museum-cum-cultural
centre, due for completion in
2010. In 2001 a whole swath of
late-medieval Barcelona, which

had been flattened to make way
for the sinister Ciutadella fortress
(see p178) in the 18th century, was
discovered here.

### MUSEU BARBIER-MUELLER D'ART PRECOLOMBÍ

☎ 93 310 45 16; www.barbier-mueller
.ch; Carrer de Montcada 12-14; adult/under
16yr/senior & student €3/free/1.50,
1st Sun of month free; 🕙 11am-7pm
Tue-Fri, 10am-7pm Sat, 10am-3pm Sun &
holidays; Ⓜ Jaume I
In this branch of the prestigious
Geneva-based Barbier-Mueller
museum you'll find a sparkling
assortment of art from the pre-
Columbian civilisations of Central
and South America. Gold glitters in
the form of at times highly intricate
ornamental objects, expressive
masks and women's jewellery.
These pieces are complemented by
plenty of statuary, ceramics, textiles,
and ritual and household objects
from all over South America.

### MUSEU DE CIÈNCIES NATURALS

☎ 93 319 69 12; www.bcn.es/museu
ciencies; Passeig de Picasso s/n; adult/
concession €3.70/2.10; 🕙 10am-6.30pm
Tue-Sat, to 2.30pm Sun; Ⓜ Arc de Triomf
The Natural Sciences Museum is
two in one: the Museu de Zoologia
housed in the Castell dels Tres
Dragons (Castle of the Three
Dragons); and the Museu de Geologia.

The playful Castell dels Tres Dragons (Castle of the Three Dragons), which houses the Museu de Zoologia

The former is the more interesting half, for content and for the building itself, a caprice designed by Domènech i Montaner. The coats of arms are all invented and the whole building exudes a playful air. Inside you'll find stuffed animals, model elephants and the inevitable skeletons of huge creatures.

### MUSEU DE LA XOCOLATA
☎ 93 268 78 78; http://pastisseria.com; Plaça de Pons i Clerch s/n; adult/under 7yr €3.90/free, 1st Mon of month free; 10am-7pm Mon & Wed-Sat, to 3pm Sun & holidays; M Jaume I
Explore the sticky story of chocolate through audiovisual displays (in English on request), touch-screen presentations, historical exhibits and the most extraordinary chocolate models of anything from grand monuments such as La Sagrada Família to cartoon characters such as Winnie the Pooh.

### MUSEU PICASSO
☎ 93 256 30 00; www.museupicasso.bcn.es; Carrer de Montcada 15-23; adult/senior & under 16yr/student €9/free/6, temporary exhibitions €5.80/free/3, 1st Sun of month free; 10am-8pm Tue-Sun & holidays; M Jaume I
The setting alone, in five contiguous stone mansions (see p20), makes this museum worth a visit.

NEIGHBOURHOODS

LA RIBERA

This is the place to discover the formative years in the life of the genius and his extraordinary early talent. The Blue Period is well represented.

## ◎ PALAU DE LA MÚSICA CATALANA

☎ 902 475485; www.palaumusica .org; Carrer de Sant Francesc de Paula 2; adult/child/student incl guided tour €10/free/9; ⏰ 10am-6pm Easter & Aug, to 3.30pm Sep-Jul; Ⓜ Urquinaona
The Palace of Catalan Music drips with all the fevered imagination that Modernista architect Lluís

Domènech i Montaner could muster for it. Finished in 1908, its acoustics were lousy, but this World Heritage gem remains an enchanting concert setting. In 2004 a new auditorium and out-door cafe were added. The exterior and foyer are opulent, but are nothing compared with the inte-rior of the main auditorium. Tours (50 minutes) run every half-hour.

## ◎ PARC DE LA CIUTADELLA

Passeig de Picasso; ⏰ 8am-9pm Apr-Sep, to 8pm Oct & Mar, to 6pm Nov-Feb; Ⓜ Arc de Triomf or Barceloneta

Catalonia's imposing regional parliament building, located in Parc de la Ciutadella

Stroll, punt on the little lake or snooze in verdant Parc de la Ciutadella, site of Catalonia's regional parliament, the city zoo (below), a couple of museums (p78) and the monumental Cascada (waterfall) created in 1875–81 by Josep Fontsère with the help of a young Gaudí. The park was created when the hated 18th-century Ciutadella fortress, built by Madrid to keep watch over the restless population (see p178), was demolished.

### ZOO DE BARCELONA
☎ 93 225 67 80; www.zoobarcelona.com; entrances on Passeig de Picasso & Carrer de Wellington; adult/under 4yr/senior/4-12yr €15.40/free/8.15/9.30; ☻ 10am-7pm Jun-Sep, to 6pm mid-Mar–May & Oct, to 5pm Nov–mid-Mar; Ⓜ Barceloneta
As thrilling or depressing as any other, this small zoo occupies the southern end of the Parc de la Ciutadella and boasts 7500 creatures great and small. Plans are afoot to create another zoo on

the waterfront in Parc del Fòrum (p100), but it appears this one will remain in action in one form or another whatever happens.

## 🛍 SHOP
Two themes stand out for your shopping basket: hip young fashion around Carrer del Rec; and that fashion's deadly enemy – food, glorious food. From coffee beans to cheese, fine wines to assorted sausages, mouth-watering options abound within waddling distance of the Santa Maria del Mar church.

### 🛍 ARLEQUÍ MÀSCARES
*Masks*
☎ 93 268 27 52; www.arlequimask.com; Carrer de la Princesa 7; ☻ 10.30am-8pm Mon-Sat, to 4pm Sun; Ⓜ Jaume I
A little house of horrors (or delights, depending on your mood), this shop specialises in masks to wear and for decoration. Stock also includes a beautiful range of decorative boxes in Catalan themes.

### 🛍 CASA GISPERT *Food & Drink*
☎ 93 319 75 35; www.casagispert .com in Catalan; Carrer dels Sombrerers 23; ☻ 9.30am-2pm & 4-7.30pm Tue-Fri, 10am-2pm & 5-8pm Sat; Ⓜ Jaume I
Nuts and coffee are roasted in a 19th-century wood-fired oven at this wonderfully aromatic wholesaler. Hazelnuts and almonds are

Roasted coffee and nuts at Casa Gispert (p81)

the specialities, complemented by piles of dried fruit and a host of artisanal products, such as mustards and preserves.

### 🏠 CUSTO BARCELONA *Fashion*

☎ 93 268 78 93; www.custo-barcelona
.com; Plaça de les Olles 7; ☷ 10am-10pm
Mon-Sat; Ⓜ Barceloneta

Created in the early 1980s by the Dalmau brothers, Custo is the biggest name in contemporary Barcelona fashion and one of its trendiest exports. The dazzling colours and cuts of anything from dinner jackets to hot pants are for the uninhibited. It has five other outlets around town.

### 🏠 EL MAGNÍFICO *Food & Drink*

☎ 93 319 60 81; www.cafeselmag
nifico.com; Carrer de l'Argenteria 64;
☷ 9.30am-2pm & 4-8pm Mon-Fri,
9.30am-2pm Sat; Ⓜ Jaume I

Take a veritable tour of world coffee with the friendly Sans family. They had so much fun with their beans and blends that they opened another store across the street, **Sans & Sans** (Carrer de l'Argenteria 59), devoted to more than 200 types of tea.

### 🏠 LA BOTIFARRERIA
*Food & Drink*

☎ 93 319 91 23; Carrer de Santa Maria 4;
☷ 8.30am-2.30pm & 5-8.30pm Mon-Fri,
8.30am-3pm Sat; Ⓜ Jaume I

As they say, 'sausages with imagination'! Although this delightful deli sells all sorts of cheeses, hams, fresh hamburger patties, snacks and other goodies, the mainstay is an astounding variety of handcrafted sausages. Not just the pork variety, but those stuffed with anything from orange and onion to apple curry!

### 🏠 LA GALERÍA DE SANTA MARÍA NOVELLA
*Perfumes, Herbs*

☎ 93 268 02 37; www.lagaleria
-smnovella.com in Spanish; Carrer de
l'Espaseria 4-8; Ⓜ Jaume I

If you've visited Florence you may have encountered the wonderful medieval pharmacy, the Officina

Profuma-Farmaceutica di Santa Maria Novella. Known for its all-natural perfumes, lotions and herbal remedies, it has become a worldwide phenomenon. How about a bottle of 'aromatic vinegar of the seven thieves'?

## 🅾 OLISOLIVA
*Food & Drink*

☎ 93 268 14 72; www.olisoliva.com in Spanish; Avinguda de Francesc Cambó s/n; 🕙 9am-2pm Mon, 9am-3.30pm Tue, Wed & Sat, 9am-3.30pm & 5-8.30pm Thu & Fri; Ⓜ Jaume I

Inside the Mercat de Santa Caterina (p78), this simple store is stacked with olive oils and vinegars from all over Spain. Taste some of the products before deciding. Some of the best olive oils come from southern Spain, and the owners will be happy to explain the wonders of any number of their products (many of which come from abroad, too).

## 🅾 OUTLET *Fashion*

☎ 93 268 72 49; Carrer de l'Esparteria 12; 🕙 11am-2.30pm & 4.30-9pm Mon-Fri, 11am-9pm Sat; Ⓜ Barceloneta

Discounted fashions from the previous year from designers like Hugo Boss, G-Star, Armani Jeans and Viktor & Rolf find their way into this chaotic store, where you can look forward to markdowns of up to half price.

## 🅾 TALLER ANTIC
*Silver, Glassware*

☎ 93 310 73 03; Carrer de la Princesa 14; 🕙 10.15am-8pm; Ⓜ Jaume I

Step back in time and place as you handle the delicate silver and glassware. Old-style perfume bottles, and the kind of accessories ladies and gents might have used in the 19th century, make this a nostalgic's corner of paradise.

## 🅾 TOT FORMATGE
*Food & Drink*

☎ 93 319 53 75; Passeig del Born 13; 🕙 5-8pm Mon, 9am-2pm & 5-8pm Tue-Fri, 10.30am-1.30pm Sat; Ⓜ Jaume I

Some gifts can certainly be a little cheesy, and none more so than the olfactory offerings in this All Cheese locale. A powerful assembly of the best in Spanish and European cheeses is on display, and little platters with samples of the products are scattered about the store.

## 🅾 VILA VINITECA
*Food & Drink*

☎ 93 268 32 27; www.vilaviniteca .es in Spanish; Carrer dels Agullers 7; 🕙 8.30am-8.30pm Mon-Sat; Ⓜ Jaume I

This unassuming shop has a superb range of Spanish and international wines, from cheap table varieties to vintage treasures, sold by enthusiastic staff. They know their stuff, having been in the booze business since 1932. At No 9 they have

## Carles Abellán
*Owner and head chef of Comerç 24 (opposite) and Tapaç 24 (p123)*

**You started at a restaurant in El Poblenou…** I was a waiter but I told them, 'put me in the kitchen or I'm off!' And they did – washing dishes. **Four years later you started at El Bulli…** I spent 16 years working with Ferran Adrià. **It seems that Barcelona, and Spain, have been at the forefront of a cuisine revolution.** We have taken gigantic steps. That's natural, because 20 years ago we were *so* far behind. Now things are evening out. The differences are not so great between Spain and elsewhere. **Why would a 'molecular cook' open a tapas bar (Tapaç 24)?** I like rock, classical music and hip-hop. It's the same with food. I love eating at Bar Pinotxo (p67). I love paella, Chinese, everything! I even like molecular cuisine. There are two types of cooking: good and bad.

another store devoted to gourmet food products, with a restaurant downstairs.

# 🍴 EAT

Although restaurants pop up all over La Ribera, the greatest concentration is in the area southeast of Carrer de la Princesa.

### 🍴 BAR DEL CONVENT *Cafe* €

☎ 93 310 37 32; Carrer del Comerç 36; 🕑 9am-10pm Mon-Thu, 9am-midnight Fri, 10am-midnight Sat; Ⓜ Arc de Triomf
Set amid the fragile-looking but beautiful remains of the Gothic cloister of the one-time Convent de Sant Agustí (most of the grounds of which are now used as a civic centre), this is a pleasant cafe for a cuppa, a tipple and/or some cake and snacks.

### 🍴 BUBÓ *Tapas* €€

☎ 93 268 72 24; www.bubo.ws; Carrer de les Caputxes 6 & 10; 🕑 4pm-midnight Mon, 10am-midnight Tue-Thu & Sun, 10am-2am Fri & Sat; Ⓜ Jaume I; ⊠ Ⓥ
Pastry chef Carles Mampel operates an exquisite shop and, next door, a small restaurant where you wade through a phalanx of tapas and small savoury dishes to get down to the serious business of trying out his devilish desserts. Try the set lunch menu, which consists of a couple of *amuse-gueules* and six savoury tapas (€16).

### 🍴 CAL PEP *Tapas* €€–€€€

☎ 93 310 79 61; www.calpep.com; Plaça de les Olles 8; 🕑 lunch & dinner Tue-Fri, dinner Mon, lunch Sat, closed Easter & Aug; Ⓜ Barceloneta; ⊠
This boisterous tapas bar brims with energy and personality thanks to Pep, the owner and chef. Get here early for squeezing space at the bar and gourmet bar snacks, such as *cloïsses amb pernil* (clams and ham – seriously! – at €12). For one of the handful of tables out back, book a long way ahead.

### 🍴 CENTRE CULTURAL EUSKAL ETXEA *Basque* €€

☎ 93 310 21 85; Placeta de Montcada 1; 🕑 lunch & dinner Tue-Sat, lunch Sun; Ⓜ Jaume I; ♿
One of the more established Basque tapas bars in Barcelona, this cultural centre still beats many of its flashier newcomer competitors for authenticity and atmosphere. Choose your *pintxos* (snacks), sip *txacoli* wine, and keep the tooth picks so the staff can count them up and work out your bill. You could almost be in San Sebastián.

### 🍴 COMERÇ 24 *Modern* €€€

☎ 93 319 21 02; www.carlesabellan .com; Carrer del Comerç 24; 🕑 lunch & dinner Tue-Sat; Ⓜ Arc de Triomf; ⊠
In the vanguard of Barcelona's modern eateries, this place is a witches' den of almost infernal

NEIGHBOURHOODS

LA RIBERA

variety and extremes. The decor is unremittingly black, the owner-chef Carles Abellán a Ferran Adrià alumnus and the cuisine eclectic. The emphasis is on waves of bite-sized snacks that traverse the culinary globe.

### ☷ EL XAMPANYET
*Tapas* €-€€

☎ 93 319 70 03; Carrer de Montcada 22; ☾ lunch & dinner Tue-Sat, lunch Sun; Ⓜ Jaume I

As you emerge from the museums on this street, you might be snared by the smell of anchovies wafting out of this colourful, old-time *cava* (Spanish sparkling wine) bar. It's worth a visit more for the timeless setting of colourful tiled walls and convivial timber benches than for the cooking.

### ☷ GRAVIN *Italian* €€
☎ 93 268 46 28; Carrer Rera Palau 3; ☾ dinner Mon & Tue, lunch & dinner Wed-Sun; Ⓜ Barceloneta

A two-brother team from Puglia in southern Italy runs this pleasant trattoria, where you can be sure to find orecchiette (ear-shaped pasta), risotto with mushrooms and gorgonzola cheese, and interesting items such as lemon spaghetti. Oven-cooked fish is a star and the homemade *panna cotta* quivers in anticipation of its impending ingestion. Italians, very hard to please outside their home country, have been seen to exit with satisfied grins.

### ☷ IKIBANA *Japanese* €€
☎ 93 295 67 32; www.ikibana.es; Passeig de Picasso 32; ☾ lunch & dinner; Ⓜ Barceloneta

Check out the atmosphere at tapas bar El Xampanyet

## GETTING LOST DOWN CARRER DELS BANYS VELLS

The heavy stone walls along this narrow street (D4), which runs northwest away from the Església de Santa Maria del Mar, ooze centuries of history. Indeed, the street is named after the old public baths located here in medieval times. Various inviting restaurants, bars and shops are found here – everything from a Cuban diner to an African art shop.

It feels like you are walking on water as you enter this Japanese-fusion lounge affair. A broad selection of makis, tempuras, sushi and more is served at high tables with leather-backed stools. The wide-screen TV switches from chilled music clips to live shots of the kitchen whence your wasabi wandered.

### 🍴 ORÍGEN *Catalan* €

☎ 93 310 75 31; Carrer de la Vidrieria 6-8; 🕑 12.30pm-1am; Ⓜ Jaume I; 🔀
A treasure chest of Catalan regional products, this place has become a popular chain of restaurants offering nicely presented bite-sized dishes (mostly around €5 to €8), like *ànec amb naps* (duck and turnip) or *civet de senglar* (jugged boar), that you mix and match over wine by the glass.

### 🍴 PLA DE LA GARSA
*Catalan* €€

☎ 93 315 24 13; Carrer dels Assaonadors 13; 🕑 dinner; Ⓜ Jaume I; 🔀
This staunchly Catalan restaurant was Barcelona's hippest hang-out during the twilight of Franco's reign. Scattered with antiques and original 19th-century fixtures, the 17th-century house remains enchanting. Try the enticing *tast selecte*, a copious tasting menu.

### 🍴 SET (7) PORTES *Catalan* €€

☎ 93 319 30 33; www.7portes.com; Passeig d'Isabel II 14; 🕑 1pm-1am; Ⓜ Barceloneta; 🔀
Gilt-framed mirrors, black-and-white-tiled floors and somewhat gruff 'service' are hallmarks of this Barcelona classic, founded in 1836. Once beloved of celebs and still famous for paella, it serves seafood platters and huge portions.

### 🍴 TANTARANTANA
*Mediterranean* €€

☎ 93 268 24 10; Carrer d'En Tantarantana 24; 🕑 dinner Mon-Sat; Ⓜ Jaume I or Arc de Triomf
There is something comforting about the old-style marble-top tables, upon which you can sample simple but well-prepared dishes such as risotto or grilled tuna served with vegetables and ginger. It attracts an early-30-something

## BAR-HOPPING ALONG PASSEIG DEL BORN

Short, leafy, cobbled Passeig del Born (E4) is the thumping heart of the nightlife that spreads out along the streets and lanes here. There's no need to single out any place along this street – they've all got a great atmosphere. Starting at the apse of Església de Santa Maria del Mar, a series of similarly good stops stretches along the left flank. Miramelindo (No 15) is a heaving barn, followed by the cosier Bermibau (No 17) with its wicker chairs and cocktails. El Copetín (No 19) and No Sé (No 21) are also good. Across the road, head for the tiny upstairs section of Pitin (No 34). For ground-level people-watching, pull up a stool at the streetfront window of Cactus, across the road from Pitín at No 32.

crowd, who also enjoy the outdoor seating in summer.

### 🍴 WUSHU Asian €€

☎ 93 310 73 13; www.wushu-restaurant.com; Avinguda del Marquès de l'Argentera 1; 🕑 1pm-midnight Tue-Sat, lunch Sun; Ⓜ Barceloneta; ✗

This Australian-run wok restaurant serves up an assortment of tasty pan-Asian dishes, including pad thai, curries and more. What about kangaroo *yakisoba*? Wash it down with Tiger beer. Pull up a pew at the nut-brown tables or sit at the bar.

## 🍸 DRINK

The bulk of the drinking action takes place on and around Passeig del Born. Indeed, to most people, going to El Born is synonymous with late nights.

### 🍸 BARROC Bar

☎ 93 268 46 23; Carrer del Rec 67; 🕑 3pm-2.30am Sun-Thu, 4pm-3am Fri & Sat; Ⓜ Barceloneta

With its plush, velvety lounges and stools, cherubs on the wall, and elaborate chandeliers, this spacious bar fills with punters who usually settle in for a long night's festivities. Music is downtempo early on, switching more to house in the wee hours. It often hosts live music and stages photo or video-art exhibitions.

### 🍸 DIOBAR Bar

☎ 93 319 56 19; Avinguda del Marquès de l'Argentera 27; 🕑 10pm-3am; Ⓜ Barceloneta

A basement DJ bar with oomph, Diobar has become one of the most popular preclub dance spots in El Born. Generally the vibe is house and deep house. Not a few of the friends you make here will head off to Catwalk (p102) after closing.

### 🍸 GIMLET Cocktail Bar

☎ 93 310 10 27; Carrer del Rec 24; 🕑 10pm-3am; Ⓜ Jaume I

Transport yourself to a Humphrey Bogart movie, almost. The punters in this timeless cocktail bar seem to get younger and grungier all the time, but the cocktails (around €8) remain the same, and somehow this simple little bar (started by the city's star cocktail-maker, Javier Muelas) continues to exert a quiet, if smoky, magnetism.

### ▼ LA FIANNA *Bar*
☎ 93 315 18 10; www.lafianna.com; Carrer dels Banys Vells 15; ⏰ 7pm-2am Mon-Wed, 7pm-3am Thu-Sat, 2-11pm Sun; Ⓜ Jaume I

There is something medieval-Oriental about this bar, with its bare stone walls, forged-iron candelabras and cushion-covered lounges. It heaves with punters and as the night wears on it's elbow room only. It offers snack food, too.

### ▼ LA VINYA DEL SENYOR *Wine Bar*
☎ 93 310 33 79; Plaça de Santa Maria del Mar 5; ⏰ noon-1am Tue-Sun; Ⓜ Jaume I

A wine-taster's fantasy, this bar has a stunning location looking out over the Església de Santa Maria del Mar. You can choose from almost 300 varieties of wine and *cava* from around the world, and enjoy inventive *platillos* (mini-tapas) as you sip your drink. Try to grab the table by the window upstairs.

## ☆ PLAY

### ☆ PALAU DE LA MÚSICA CATALANA *Live Music*
☎ 902 475485; www.palaumusica.org; Carrer de Sant Francesc de Paula 2; admission €10-150; ⏰ box office 10am-9pm Mon-Sat, 1hr before performance Sun; Ⓜ Urquinaona

Aside from being a beacon of Modernisme (see p80), this multi-use venue hosts an eclectic musical program, in both the stunning main theatre and the smaller, modern chamber-orchestra auditorium. It has an excellent cafe, too.

# >PORT VELL & LA BARCELONETA

Where La Rambla meets the Med, Port Vell (Old Port) stands as pretty testimony to the city's transformation since the 1980s. You can shoot up the Columbus monument for bird's-eye views of the posh marina, World Trade Center, Maremàgnum shopping and entertainment complex, and giant aquarium. You should get an inside view of the aquarium too, especially the shark tunnel.

Just beyond stretches the 18th-century, working-class waterfront district of La Barceloneta. It was laid out by military engineer Juan Martín Cermeño to replace housing destroyed to make way for the Ciutadella fortress (see p178). The cute houses along narrow streets were later subdivided into four separate 30-sq-metre abodes and subsequently converted into six-storey rabbit warrens. The attentive eye will pick out some of the few remaining original houses.

What had become an industrial slum by the end of the 19th century is today in the grip of gradual gentrification. But La Barceloneta's grid of narrow lanes still have an earthy feel, and countless seafood eateries lurk in this labyrinth. On the west side of the district boats bob in another chic marina, while the seaside beach, with its summer bars and contented buzz, is a polyglot *Who's Who* of European sun-seekers.

## PORT VELL & LA BARCELONETA

### ◎ SEE
Edifici de Gas Natural.....1 E2
Golondrina Excursion
  Boats .......................2 B5
L'Aquàrium ..................3 D4
Monument a Colom........4 B4
Museu d'Història de
  Catalunya.................5 D3
Museu Marítim..............6 A5
Transbordador Aeri ......7 D5

### ◎ SHOP
Maremàgnum ...............8 C5

### ◎ EAT
Can Maño .....................9 E3
El Vaso de Oro.............10 D2
Suquet de l'Almirall .....11 E4
Torre d'Alta Mar..........12 D5

### ◎ DRINK
Santa Marta ................13 E4

### ◎ PLAY
Club Natació Atlètic-
  Barcelona ................14 E5
Mondo .......................15 C4
Poliesportiu Marítim....16 F1

Please see over for map

# ◎ SEE

The star attractions, apart from simply lazing the day away at the beach, are l'Aquàrium and its shark tunnel, and the fascinating Museu Marítim, housed in the city's former medieval shipyards.

### ◎ EDIFICI DE GAS NATURAL
**Passeig de Salvat Papasseit;**
Ⓜ **Barceloneta**
While only 100m high, this shimmering glass waterfront tower – designed by Enric Miralles – is extraordinary for its mirrorlike surface and weirdly protruding adjunct buildings, which could be giant glass cliffs bursting from the main tower's flank.

### ◎ GOLONDRINA EXCURSION BOATS
☎ **93 442 31 06; www.lasgolondrinas .com; Moll de les Drassanes; adult/under 4yr/4-10yr/student & senior €10.50/ free/4.80/7.70;** Ⓜ **Drassanes**

Rebecca Horn's *Homenatge a la Barceloneta*

Kids will love the 1½-hour jaunt around the harbour and along the beaches to the northeast tip of town aboard a *golondrina* (swallow). Shorter trips are also available (and tend to leave more often). If you just want to pootle around the port, there's the 35-minute **excursion** (adult/under 4yr/4-10yr €5/free/2.50) to the breakwater and back.

### ◎ L'AQUÀRIUM
☎ **93 221 74 74; www.aquariumbcn.com; Moll d'Espanya; adult/under 4yr/4-12yr/ over 60yr €16/free/11/12.50;** ☀ **9.30am-11pm daily Jul & Aug, to 9.30pm daily Jun & Sep, to 9pm Mon-Fri, to 9.30pm Sat & Sun Oct-May;** Ⓜ **Drassanes**
You won't come much closer to a set of shark choppers. The

---

### BEACHED BOXES
American Rebecca Horn's striking tribute to La Barceloneta, *Homenatge a la Barceloneta* (E4) is an eye-catching column of rusted-iron-and-glass cubes on Platja de Sant Sebastià. Erected in 1992, it pays homage to the beach bars and restaurants that disappeared around the time of the Olympic Games.

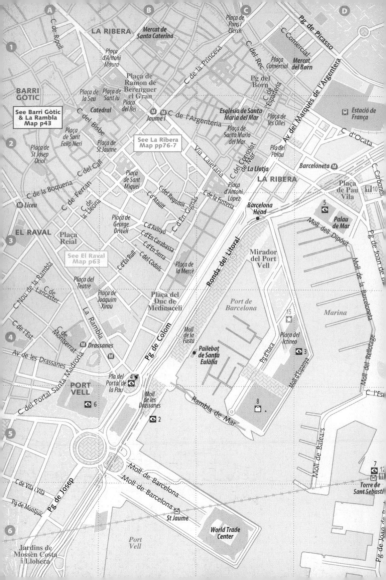

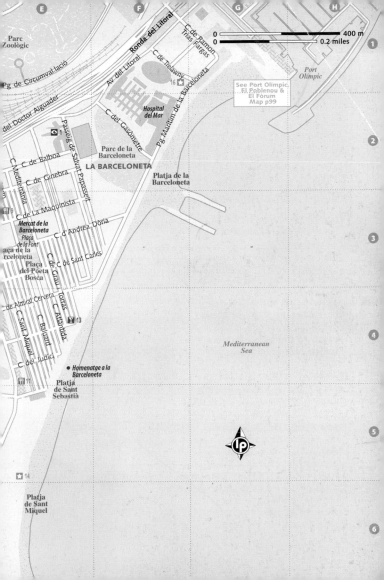

**E**

Parc
Zoològic

Pg de Circumval·lació

del Doctor Aiguader

Passeig de Salvat Papasseit

C. de Balboa

C. de Ginebra

C. Mediterrània

**LA BARCELONETA**

9

**Mercat de la
Barceloneta**

Plaça
de la Font

aça de
rceloneta

Plaça
del Poeta
Bosca

C. de Sant Carles

C. de Grau Torras

C. d'Andrea Dòria

C. de La Maquinista

de Almirall Cerveta

C. Sant Miquel

Balvard

Atlàntida

13

C. del Judici

● Homenatge a la
Barceloneta

11

**Platja
de Sant
Sebastià**

14

**Platja
de Sant
Miquel**

**F**

Ronda del Litoral

C. de Trelawny

Av. del Litoral

Pg. Marítim de la Barceloneta

**Hospital
del Mar**

16

C. del Casonette

Parc de la
Barceloneta

Platja de la
Barceloneta

**G**

C. de Ramon
Trias Fargas

0                    400 m
0              0.2 miles

See Port Olímpic,
El Poblenou &
El Fórum
Map p99

**H**

Port
Olímpic

1

2

3

*Mediterranean
Sea*

4

LP

5

6

### ART POPS UP IN PORT VELL

Designed by the American pop artist Roy Lichtenstein in 1992, the 14m *Barcelona Head* sculpture (C3), just back from Port Vell at the end of Passeig de Colom, sparkles like a ceramic comic when the sun strikes its *trencadís* (broken-tile) coating, believed to be a homage to Gaudí.

80m-long shark tunnel is the high point in this, one of Europe's largest aquariums. Some 11,000 fish (including about a dozen sharks) have become permanent residents here in an area filled with 4.5 million litres of water. The restless sharks are accompanied by splendid flapping rays and huge sunfish. Other tanks are devoted to the delights of the Red Sea, the Caribbean, Hawaii, Australia and the South Seas.

### ◎ MONUMENT A COLOM

☎ 93 302 52 24; Pla del Portal de la Pau; lift adult/under 4yr/senior & 4-12yr €2.50/free/1.50; ☽ 9am-8.30pm Jun-Sep, 10am-6.30pm Oct-May; Ⓜ Drassanes

Centuries after he stumbled across the Americas, Columbus was honoured with this 60m monument, built for the Universal Exhibition in 1888. It looks like he's urging the tourists to go elsewhere, but you can catch a lift to the soles of his feet for a fine view.

### ◎ MUSEU D'HISTÒRIA DE CATALUNYA

☎ 93 225 47 00; www.mhcat.net; Plaça de Pau Vila 3; adult/senior & under 7yr/student €4/free/3, 1st Sun of month free; ☽ 10am-7pm Tue & Thu-Sat, to 8pm Wed, to 2.30pm Sun & holidays; Ⓜ Barceloneta

From the caves of the Pyrenees to air-raid shelters of the civil war, this hectic but entertaining interactive display shows how Catalans and other folk (including Romans and Arabs) have rolled with history's ups and downs over 2000 years. Pick up a guide in English at reception and don't miss the view from the top-floor restaurant.

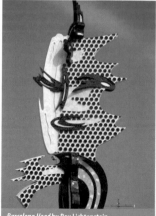

*Barcelona Head* by Roy Lichtenstein

### 🎥 MUSEU MARÍTIM

☎ 93 342 99 20; www.mmb.cat;
Avinguda de les Drassanes; adult/under
7yr/senior & student €6.50/free/3.25,
3-8pm 1st Sat of month free; ⏰ 10am-
8pm; Ⓜ Drassanes

Much of Barcelona's medieval
prosperity depended on sea
trade. In these one-time Gothic
shipyards, you can get a sense
of the glory and adventure of
centuries of maritime history (see
p24), from the era of rafts to the
age of steam. Entry also gives you
access to the 1918 three-master
**Pailebot de Santa Eulàlia**, moored at
Port Vell (C4).

### 🎥 TRANSBORDADOR AERI

Passeig Escullera; one way/return
€9/12.50; ⏰ 11am-8pm mid-Jun–mid-
Sep, 10.45am-7pm Mar–mid-Jun &
mid-Sep–late Oct, 10.30am-5.45pm late
Oct-Feb; Ⓜ Barceloneta or 🚌 17, 39,
57 or 64

This cable car (aka *funicular aeri*),
strung out precariously across the
harbour to Montjuïc, provides a
bird's-eye view of the city. The
cabins float between Miramar
(Montjuïc) and the Torre de Sant
Sebastià (La Barceloneta).

## 🛍 SHOP

### 🛒 MAREMÀGNUM
*Shopping Mall*

☎ 93 225 81 00; www.maremagnum
.es; Moll d'Espanya s/n; ⏰ 10am-10pm
Mon-Sat; Ⓜ Drassanes

A busy mall on the water,
Maremàgnum offers an assortment of shops, bars and eateries
over several floors. At FC Botiga
on the ground floor you'll find FC
Barcelona strips and other football
souvenirs. Or perhaps sexy wom-
en's underwear at the Love Store
is more your thing. The list is long!

## 🍴 EAT

The lanes of La Barceloneta are
liberally sprinkled with eateries of
all descriptions, although seafood

---

### PORTSIDE MEANDER ALONG PASSEIG DE JOAN DE BORBÓ

Maybe it's a good thing the Metro doesn't reach the beach at La Barceloneta, obliging you to walk down the sunny portside promenade of Passeig de Joan de Borbó (E4). Megayachts sway gently on your right as you bowl down a street crackling with activity. Folks chomp cheerfully at pavement terraces, with eateries ranging from kebab stands to century-old seafood joints. King of the lot is Suquet de l'Almirall (p96). In among them you'll pass a popular UK-style pub, the Fastnet (No 22), a couple of ice-cream parlours, three shoe stores and a handy little supermarket for beach supplies.

## SEAFOOD AT THE PALAU DE MAR

The beautifully restored portside warehouses of the Palau de Mar (D3) are not just home to the intriguing Museu d'Història de Catalunya (p94). Facing the bobbing yachts is a series of five seafood restaurants, all with sunny terraces. Prices range from €35 to €40 per head and locals change their minds constantly about which (if any) are worthy of their custom, but there are few more pleasant spots to peel prawns.

is the predominant theme. So get in there and explore!

### 🍴 CAN MAÑO *Spanish* €

☎ 93 319 30 82; Carrer del Baluard 12; 🕑 lunch & dinner Mon-Sat; Ⓜ Barceloneta; ✗

Refugees from fashionable food in search of a hearty feed and a bottle of cold *turbio* (a cloudy and pleasing white wine) huddle on the communal benches here and get stuck into *raciones* (saucer-sized serves) of all sorts of seafood and other goodies. A long-lived, no-nonsense family business, it generally attracts queues…

### 🍴 EL VASO DE ORO *Tapas* €-€€

☎ 93 319 30 98; Carrer de Balboa 6; 🕑 11am-midnight; Ⓜ Barceloneta; ✗

If you like noisy, crowded bars, high-speed bar staff always ready with a smile and a wisecrack, a cornucopia of tapas, and the illusion, in here at least, that Barcelona hasn't changed in decades, come to the sassy 'Glass of Gold' on the edge of La Barceloneta. The tapas are delicious and they

brew their own German-style beers.

### 🍴 SUQUET DE L'ALMIRALL *Seafood* €€

☎ 93 221 62 33; Passeig de Joan de Borbó 65; 🕑 lunch & dinner Tue-Sat, lunch Sun; Ⓜ Barceloneta or 🚌 17, 39, 57 or 64; ✗

The order of the day is simply top-class seafood. House specialities include *arròs a la barca* (rice laden with various types of fish, squid and tomato) and *suquet* (seafood stew).

### 🍴 TORRE D'ALTA MAR *Mediterranean* €€€

☎ 93 221 00 07; www.torredealtamar .com; Torre de Sant Sebastià, Passeig de Joan de Borbó 88; 🕑 lunch & dinner Tue-Sat, dinner Sun & Mon; Ⓜ Barceloneta or 🚌 17, 39, 57 or 64; ✗

The aerial views from the top of this metal tower make it the most spectacular dining setting in town. Seafood dominates the menu, the wine list is strong, and the food and service are generally good. It is the perfect spot for a romantic dinner for two.

# ▼ DRINK

## ▼ SANTA MARTA *Bar*

**Carrer de Guitert 60;** ✆ **10.30am-7pm Sun, Mon, Wed & Thu, to 10pm Fri & Sat;** Ⓜ **Barceloneta or** 🚌 **45, 57, 59 or 157**
This take-it-easy, seaside bar was made for its young, travelling crowd – the kind who have elected to hang out in Barcelona for a stretch in search of themselves or until their pennies run out. Have a light meal, sip a summertime beer outside or cosy up for a coffee in winter at the tiny tables inside.

# ★ PLAY

## ★ CLUB NATACIÓ ATLÈTIC-BARCELONA *Swimming*

☎ **93 221 00 10; www.cnab.org; Plaça de Mar s/n; adult/under 10yr €10.10/5.85;** ✆ **6.30am-11pm Mon-Fri, 7am-11pm Sat year-round, 8am-5pm Sun & holidays Oct–mid-May, 8am-8pm Sun & holidays mid-May–Sep;** Ⓜ **Barceloneta or** 🚌 **17, 39, 57 or 64;** 🚼
Down near La Barceloneta beach, this athletic club has one indoor and two outdoor pools. Of the outdoor offerings, one is heated for lap swimming during winter. The admission charge includes use of the gym and private beach access.

## ★ MONDO *Club*

**www.mondobcn.com; Moll d'Espanya; admission €9;** ✆ **midnight-5am Wed-Sun;** Ⓜ **Barceloneta**
Perched on the floor above the Imax cinema and doubling as a restaurant, Mondo has quickly etched a name for itself in the diaries of Barcelona clubbers. Aside from the main dance area – for anything from R&B on Thursday to deep house on Saturday (with some concessions to '80s hits en route) – you can also enjoy the water views from the terrace. It attracts a good-looking, predominantly 30-something crowd.

## ★ POLIESPORTIU MARÍTIM *Swimming, Thalassotherapy*

☎ **93 224 04 40; www.claror.cat in Catalan; Passeig Marítim de la Barceloneta 33-35; admission Mon-Fri €14.40, Sat, Sun & holidays €17;** ✆ **7am-midnight Mon-Fri, 8am-9pm Sat, 8am-4pm Sun & holidays;** Ⓜ **Ciutadella Vila Olímpica**
Water babies will squeal with delight in this thalassotherapeutic (sea-water therapy) sports centre. Apart from the smallish swimming pool, there is a labyrinth of hot, warm and freezing-cold spa pools, along with thundering waterfalls that are wonderful for some massage relief.

# >PORT OLÍMPIC, EL POBLENOU & EL FÒRUM

Strolling, skating or riding your bicycle northeast from the beaches of La Barceloneta, you'll reach Port Olímpic, a crammed marina that was created for the 1992 Olympics. It is lined by heaving if largely tacky bars and eateries. Barcelona's classiest hotel stands here, too.

Inland, the southwest end of El Poblenou, a one-time industrial workers' district, was converted into the Vila Olímpica, modern apartments that housed athletes and were sold off after the Olympics. Now, the rest of El Poblenou is being transformed in an ambitious urban regeneration scheme. At its heart is the planned hi-tech zone, 22@bcn. Its symbol is Barcelona's most spectacular modern architectural icon, Jean Nouvel's Torre Agbar. But plenty of other glittering new buildings are going up as the city attempts to draw in cutting-edge companies from around the world.

El Poblenou's waterfront is lined by the city's better beaches, which spread northeast towards Barcelona's other major development project, El Forùm. Amid high-rise apartments and luxury hotels lies Parc del Fòrum. Dominated by the weird, triangular Edifici Fòrum, it comes to life in summer with a protected bathing area, kids' playgrounds and major concerts. A zoo is also (slowly) being built by the sea. As a new pole of residential and business activity, El Fòrum has not been a runaway success, but much life has been breathed into a once largely abandoned part of the city.

## PORT OLÍMPIC, EL POBLENOU & EL FÒRUM

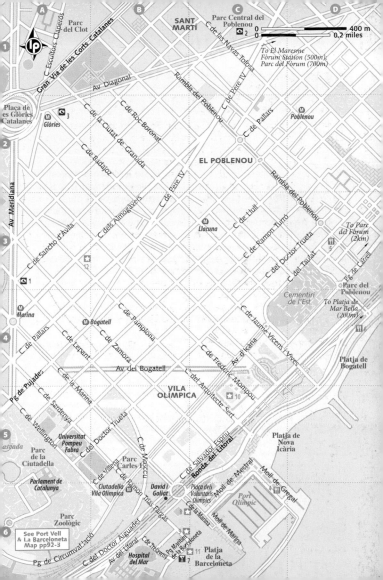

NEIGHBOURHOODS

PORT OLÍMPIC, EL POBLENOU & EL FÒRUM

# 👁 SEE

There are no major sights in this area – most people come here for the beaches. A few key objects are worth keeping your eye on, however.

## 👁 MUSEU DE CARROSSES FÚNEBRES

☎ 902 076902; www.sfbsa.es; Carrer de Sancho d'Àvila 2; admission free; 🕑 10am-1pm & 4-6pm Mon-Fri, 10am-1pm Sat, Sun & holidays; Ⓜ Marina

A somewhat morbid air pervades this collection of horse-drawn hearses (and a few motorised ones) used in the city from the 18th century until the 1950s. Some are decked out with life-sized model horses and mannequins of funeral-company folk in full VIP gear of yesteryear.

## 👁 PARC CENTRAL DEL POBLENOU

Avinguda Diagonal; Ⓜ Poblenou

This odd new park, designed by Jean Nouvel, boasts stylised metal seats and statuary. Barcelona is sprinkled with parks whose principal element is cement. This one is supposed to be different, but the plants and trees won't fully bloom before 2010, so the jury is out on the result.

## 👁 PARC DEL FÒRUM

☎ 93 356 10 50; www.bcn.es/parcdel forum; Rambla de Prim 2-4; Ⓜ El Maresme Fòrum; Ⓟ

Once a wasteland around a creaky sewerage plant, the Parc del Fòrum lies at the heart of the ambitious El Fòrum urban renewal project. The **Edifici Fòrum** houses a permanent exhibition on Barcelona's urban transformation, **Barcelona Propera** (admission free; 🕑 11am-8pm Tue-Sun). The highlight is an amazingly detailed 1:1000 scale model of the city. It took 20,000 man-hours (more than five months) to create and is claimed to be the biggest such city model in Europe. The building itself, by Swiss architects Herzog & de Meuron, is a navy-blue triangular apparition that would not be out of place in a Star Trek movie. Next door, Josep Lluís Mateo's

## THEY MIGHT BE GIANTS

In the shadow of the two skyscrapers of the Vila Olímpica (Olympic Village) on Plaça dels Voluntaris Olímpics, Antoni Llena's 1993 sculpture *David i Goliat* (B6) honours the poor who were uprooted from this neighbourhood by the 1992 Olympics. It consists of a large metal sheet shaped like a mask and suspended 20m up on three steel tubes.

Go for (body) bronze at Port Olímpic

**Centre de Convencions Internacional de Barcelona** (CCIB) has capacity for 15,000 delegates. The **Zona de Banys** (☼ 11am-8pm May-Sep) bathing area has kayaks and bikes for rent.

### 🏛 TORRE AGBAR
☎ 93 342 21 29; www.torreagbar.com; **Avinguda Diagonal 225;** ☼ **10am-7pm Mon-Sat, to 2pm Sun;** Ⓜ **Glòries**
Barcelona's very own cucumber-shaped tower, Jean Nouvel's luminous Torre Agbar (headquarters of the city water company) is the most daring addition to Barcelona's skyline since the first towers of La Sagrada Família went up. Completed in 2005, it shimmers

in shades of midnight blue and lipstick red, especially at night. Temporary exhibitions (usually on a watery theme) are sometimes held in the foyer.

## 🍴 EAT
The Port Olímpic marina brims with eateries but most are mediocre. Search out these suggestions to avoid disappointment.

### 🍴 EL CANGREJO LOCO
*Seafood*                                    €€
☎ 93 221 05 33; www.elcangrejoloco .com; Moll de Gregal 29-30; ☼ lunch & dinner; Ⓜ Ciutadella Vila Olímpica; ♿
The 'Mad Crab' is the pick of the culinary crop at the Port Olímpic marina. It has sections on two levels and is always chock-full. Such fish standards as *bacallà* (cod) and *rap* (monkfish) are served in various guises and melt in the mouth, as does the *sarsuela,* a kind of fish stew (€35).

### 🍴 ELS PESCADORS
*Seafood*                                    €€
☎ 93 225 20 18; www.elspescadors .com; Plaça de Prim 1; ☼ lunch & dinner; Ⓜ Poblenou; ♿
Fresh fish brought down from coastal markets dominates the menu at this pleasing restaurant on a quiet square. Oven-baked catch of the day and gourmet cod dishes are strong cards. Eat outside

or in the timber-lined interior, the timeless tavern atmosphere of which has been maintained.

### 🍴 XIRINGUITO D'ESCRIBÀ
*Seafood, Paella* €€

☎ 93 221 07 29; www.escriba.es; Ronda del Litoral 42, Platja de Bogatell; 🕐 lunch; M Llacuna

An excellent seafront eatery (you may have to queue), Xiringuito d'Escribà is one of the few places where one person can order from the selection of paella and *fideuà* (similar to paella, but made with vermicelli noodles) – normally it's for a minimum of two people. Prices are higher than average, but the quality matches. The dessert patisseries are alone worth the trip.

## 🍸 DRINK
### 🍸 CDLC *Lounge Bar*
☎ 93 224 04 70; www.cdlcbarcelona .com; Passeig Marítim de la Barceloneta 32; 🕐 noon-3am; M Ciutadella Vila Olímpica

The Carpe Diem Lounge Club is one of the hippest *locales* on Barcelona's waterfront. Stretch out on the 'Bali' lounges, get mysterious in the Morocco space, dance away inside or sip cocktails outside to an acoustic diet of chill while gazing over the sand and sea. You can feel just as cool here for lunch or dinner (the kitchen closes and tables are cleared from the dance floor at midnight).

## ⭐ PLAY
### ⭐ CASINO DE BARCELONA
*Casino*

☎ 93 225 78 78; www.casino-barce lona.com; Carrer de la Marina 19-21; 🕐 11am-5am; M Ciutadella Vila Olímpica

Feeling lucky? If this is your night, you might manage to walk out of here with some extra cash for a bottle of *cava* (Spanish sparkling wine) in one of the nearby bars or clubs.

### ⭐ CATWALK *Club*
☎ 93 224 07 40; www.clubcatwalk.net in Spanish; Carrer de Ramon Trias Fargas 2-4; admission €15; 🕐 midnight-6am Thu-Sun; M Ciutadella Vila Olímpica

A well-dressed crowd piles in here for danceable house, occasionally mellowed down with more body-hugging electro and funk. Alternatively, sink into a fat lounge

### BEACH BARS

Scattered along Barcelona's strands is a series of hip little beach bars bringing chilled club sounds to the seaside. Sip on your favourite cocktail as you take in the day's last rays. These places keep humming from about 10am until midnight or 1am (Easter to October), depending on the forces of law and order and how good business is. Some of the best are on Platja de Mar Bella.

## SPOILED FOR CHOICE

Classic movies are sometimes shown in such diverse locations as La Pedrera (p110), Sala Apolo (p144), the L'Illa del Diagonal shopping mall (p151), Caixa-Forum (p135) and the Centre de Cultura Contemporània de Barcelona (p64). Summer screens are sometimes set up by the pool at Piscines Bernat Picornell (p144), at the Castell de Montjuïc (p135) and in the Parc del Fòrum (p100).

for a quiet tipple and whisper. Local DJ Jekey leads the way most nights.

### ⭐ ICÀRIA YELMO CINEPLEX *Cinema*

☎ 93 221 75 85; www.yelmocineplex .es in Spanish; Carrer de Salvador Espriu 61; admission €6-7; ⌚ up to 6 sessions 11am-10.30pm, plus movie after midnight Fri & Sat; Ⓜ Ciutadella Vila Olímpica

Behind Port Olímpic, this multiplex has 15 screens showing main-stream and art-house movies in the original language – the biggest such concentration in the city.

### ⭐ OPIUM MAR *Club*

☎ 902 267486; www.opiummar.com; Passeig Marítim de la Barceloneta 34; ⌚ 8pm-6am; Ⓜ Ciutadella Vila Olímpica

White, shimmering silver and dark contrasts mark the decor in this barn of a seaside dance place. It only begins to fill with a 20- and 30-something crowd from 3am and is best in summer, when you can spill outside.

### ⭐ RAZZMATAZZ *Club*

☎ 93 272 09 10; www.salarazzmatazz .com in Spanish; Carrer dels Almogàvers 122 or Carrer de Pamplona 88; admission €15; ⌚ 1-6am Fri & Sat; Ⓜ Marina or Bogatell

Five clubs are crammed into one huge warehouse space to make this one of the most popular dance destinations in town. You can enjoy anything from rock and indie to garage, techno and '60s nostalgia. Headline acts perform live regularly.

# >L'EIXAMPLE

By far the most extensive of Barcelona's districts, this sprawling grid is full of sub-identities. Almost all the city's Modernista buildings were raised in l'Eixample. The pick of them line Passeig de Gràcia, but hundreds adorn the area. Work on Gaudí's La Sagrada Família church continues.

## L'EIXAMPLE

### ○ SEE

### ⌂ SHOP

### ⑪ EAT

### ▼ DRINK

### ☆ PLAY

Please see over for map

As Barcelona's population exploded, the medieval walls were knocked down by 1856, and in 1869 work began on l'Eixample (the Extension) to fill in the open country that then lay between Barcelona and Gràcia. Building continued until well into the 20th century. Well-to-do families snapped up prime plots and raised fanciful buildings in the eclectic style of the Modernistas.

Shoppers converge on Passeig de Gràcia and La Rambla de Catalunya. At night, mainly from Thursday to Saturday, Carrer d'Aribau and nearby streets pound with nightlife as local punters let their hair down. The 'Gaixample', around Carrer del Consell de Cent and Carrer de Muntaner, is a pole of gay nightlife. Restaurants of all possible shades and shapes are scattered across the district.

# ◉ SEE

Various museums and galleries are dotted about this district, but the main attraction is wacky Modernista architecture, led by Gaudí with La Sagrada Família church and his buildings on Passeig de Gràcia.

## ◉ CASA BATLLÓ

☎ 93 216 03 66; www.casabatllo.es; Passeig de Gràcia 43; adult/student & senior €16.50/13.20; ☺ 9am-8pm; Ⓜ Passeig de Gràcia

One of the weirdest-looking concoctions to emerge from the fantastical imagination of Antoni Gaudí is this apartment block, which he renovated early in the 20th century. Locals know it as the *casa dels ossos* (house of bones) or *casa del drac* (house of the dragon) and it's not hard to see why. The balconies look like the jaws of some strange beast and the roof represents Sant Jordi (St George) and the dragon. The staircase wafts you up to the 1st floor, where everything swirls in the main salon: the ceiling is twisted into a vortex around its sunlike lamp; the doors, window and skylights are dreamy

## MODERNISME UNPACKED

Aficionados of Barcelona's Modernista heritage should consider the **Ruta del Modernisme** (www.rutadelmodernisme.com) pack. For €12 you receive a guide to 115 Modernista buildings great and small, a map and discounts of up to 50% on the main Modernista sights in Barcelona, as well as some in other municipalities around Catalonia. For €18 you get another guide and map, *Sortim*, which leads you to bars and restaurants located in Modernista buildings. Pick up the packs at one of three Centres del Modernisme: the main tourist office at Plaça de Catalunya 17, the Hospital de la Santa Creu i de Sant Pau and the Pavellons Güell in Pedralbes.

waves of wood and coloured glass. Opening hours can be shortened on occasion.

### CASA CALVET
☎ 93 412 40 12; Carrer de Casp 48; Ⓜ Urquinaona

Gaudí's first apartment block and most conventional building won him the only award of his life – the city council's prize for the best building of 1900. It's sober from the outside, but there are hints of whimsy in the ground-floor restaurant (p121).

### CASA DE LES PUNXES
Avinguda Diagonal 420; Ⓜ Verdaguer

Josep Puig i Cadafalch could have been eating too much cheese late at night when he created this neo-Gothic fantasy, built between 1903 and 1905. Officially the Casa Terrades, the building's fairytale pointed turrets earned it the nickname Casa de les Punxes (House of Spikes).

### ESGLÉSIA DE LA PURÍSSIMA CONCEPCIÓ I ASSUMPCIÓ DE NOSTRA SENYORA
Carrer de Roger de Llúria 70; ☼ 8am-1pm & 5-9pm; Ⓜ Passeig de Gràcia

Transferred here stone by stone from the old city centre between 1871 and 1888, this 14th-century church has a pretty 16th-century cloister with a peaceful garden. Behind the church is a mixed Romanesque-Gothic bell tower

The spiky turrets of the Casa de les Punxes

(11th- to 16th-century), moved from another old town church that didn't survive, the Església de Sant Miquel.

### ◎ FUNDACIÓ ANTONI TÀPIES

☎ 93 487 03 15; www.fundaciotapies .org; Carrer d'Aragó 255; adult/under 16yr/senior & student €6/free/4; 🕑 10am-8pm Tue-Sun; Ⓜ Passeig de Gràcia

This Lluís Domènech i Montaner building – considered by many to be the prototype for Modernisme, and the first in the city to be built on an iron frame – houses the experimental work of Catalonia's greatest living artist, Antoni Tàpies, as well as exhibitions by other contemporary artists. The building is crowned with coiled wire, a curious Tàpies sculpture titled *Núvol i Cadira* (Cloud and Chair). It was closed for renovation at the time of research. Check the website for updates.

### ◎ FUNDACIÓ JOAN BROSSA

☎ 93 467 69 52; www.fundaciojoan brossa.cat; Carrer de Provença 318; admission free; 🕑 10am-2pm & 3-7pm Mon-Fri; Ⓜ Diagonal

The work of Joan Brossa (1921–98) – a difficult-to-classify mix of poet, artist, theatre man; Catalan nationalist and all-round visionary – is celebrated in this basement gallery.

### ◎ FUNDACIÓ SUÑOL

☎ 93 496 10 32; www.fundaciosunol .org; Passeig de Gràcia 98; adult/conces- sion €5/2.50; 🕑 4-8pm Mon-Wed, Fri & Sat; Ⓜ Diagonal

Rotating exhibitions of portions of this private art collection offer anything from the photography of Man Ray to sculptures by Alberto Giacometti. There are some 1200 works in total, mostly from the 20th century. Plenty of Spanish artists emerge, from Picasso to Jaume Plensa.

### ◎ FUNDACIÓN FRANCISCO GODIA

www.fundacionfgodia.org; Carrer de la Diputació 250; Ⓜ Passeig de Gràcia

An intriguing mix of medieval art, ceramics and modern paintings makes up this eclectic private collection. Medieval works include wooden sculptures of the Virgin Mary and Christ taken down from the Cross, and there are paintings by such Catalan icons as Jaume Huguet and Valencia's Joaquim Sorolla. Transferred to this new address, it had not opened at the time of writing.

### ◎ HOSPITAL DE LA SANTA CREU I DE SANT PAU

☎ 902 076621; www.santpau.es; Carrer de Cartagena 167; Ⓜ Hospital de Sant Pau

A Domènech i Montaner master- piece, begun in 1901 and finished

## THE CALM OF CARRER D'ENRIC GRANADOS

Half the city's population would like to live here. Mr Granados (1867–1916), a classical musician, probably wouldn't have minded either. The pedestrianised bottom end, at Carrer de la Diputació (C5), is marked off by the **gardens** (☼ 10am-sunset Sat & Sun from Carrer de la Diputació, 10am-sunset Mon-Fri from Plaça de l'Universitat) of the Universitat de Barcelona. The banter of diners can be heard at a couple of nearby restaurants as you wander between rows of elegant apartments to the leafy (but noisy) Plaça del Doctor Letamendi (C5). From here on, one lane of traffic trickles along the rest of the street, along which are stationed more tempting eateries, until you reach Avinguda Diagonal (this end is also pedestrian-only).

by his son in 1930, this uniquely chirpy hospital is a gargantuan Modernista landmark that includes 16 lavishly decorated pavilions. Among the many artists who contributed statuary, ceramics and artwork was the prolific Eusebi Arnau. You can wander around the grounds at any time, and it is well worth the stroll up Avinguda de Gaudí from La Sagrada Família. The hospital wards have mostly been transferred to more modern facilities, and the site will eventually house a museum on medicine, Montaner and the hospital's history.

### ☉ LA PEDRERA
☎ 902 400973; www.fundaciocaixa catalunya.es; Carrer de Provença 261-265; adult/student & EU senior €9.50/5.50; ☼ 9am-8pm Mar-Oct, to 6.30pm Nov-Feb; Ⓜ Diagonal
The most extraordinary apartment block built in Barcelona was actually called Casa Milà – after its

owners – but nicknamed La Pedrera (the Stone Quarry) by bemused locals who watched Antoni Gaudí build it from 1905 to 1910. Its rippling grey stone facade looks like a cliff face sculpted by waves and wind. It is studded with 'seaweed' in the form of wrought-iron balconies. On the 4th floor, visit El Pis de la Pedrera, a re-created Modernista apartment furnished in the style a prosperous family might have enjoyed when the block was completed. The Espai Gaudí (Gaudí Space) is housed in what used to be the attic and feels like the building's ribcage. It now offers an overview of Gaudí's work. The roof is adorned with what look like giant medieval (or 21st-century!) knights. They are in fact hallucinatory chimneypots.

### ☉ LA SAGRADA FAMÍLIA
☎ 93 207 30 31; www.sagradafamilia .org; Carrer de Mallorca 401; adult/senior & student €10/8; ☼ 9am-8pm Apr-Sep, to 6pm Oct-Mar; Ⓜ Sagrada Família

Antoni Gaudí's most extraordinary creation, still years from completion, is an ever-changing magnet for visitors. Gaudí started work on La Sagrada Família in 1884. The Nativity facade was finished in 1935, nine years after his death. The following year, anarchists destroyed many of his plans. Work restarted in 1952 and the Passion facade was raised in 1976. It is characterised by bold, angular and highly controversial decorative work depicting the passion and death of Christ by sculptor Josep Maria Subirachs. Work on the Glory facade, which will be the main entrance, is underway. When finished, the enormous temple will have room for 13,000 people – the problem may be finding that many faithful. See also p10.

### ◉ MANZANA DE LA DISCORDIA

**Passeig de Gràcia; M Passeig de Gràcia**
One might be tempted to believe some wiseacre in the Barcelona town hall back in the 1900s thought it would be amusing to have the three top Modernista architects line up for posterity. On just one block of the Passeig de Gràcia are three incredibly disparate houses, collectively known as the Manzana de la Discordia (Apple, or Block, of Discord): Gaudí's gaudy Casa Batlló (p105); Puig i Cadafalch's medieval-Dutch-looking Casa Amatller at

No 41, the foyer of which can be visited; and Domènech i Montaner's more rounded Casa Lleó Morera at No 35, visible only from the outside.

### ◉ MUSEU DE LA MÚSICA

☎ 93 256 36 50; www.museumusica .bcn.cat in Catalan & Spanish; **Carrer de Padilla 155; adult/senior & student €4/free;** 🕑 **10am-9pm Sat, Sun & holidays, 11am-9pm Mon & Wed-Fri; M Monumental**
Some 500 instruments (less than a third of those held) are on show in this modern museum in l'Auditori (p126). Instruments range from a 17th-century baroque guitar, through lutes (look out for the many-stringed 1641 'archilute' from Venice), violins, Japanese kotos, sitars from India, eight organs (some dating to the 18th century) and pianos, to a varied collection of drums and other percussion instruments from across Spain and beyond. More unusual items include the *buccèn*, a snakehead-adorned brass instrument.

### ◉ MUSEU DEL PERFUM

☎ 93 216 01 21; www.museudelperfum .com; **Passeig de Gràcia 39; adult/student & senior €5/3;** 🕑 **10.30am-2pm & 4.30-8pm Mon-Fri, 11am-2pm Sat; M Passeig de Gràcia**
Out back in the Regia perfume shop, this museum features hundreds of perfume receptacles and

Palau del Baró Quadras, the gorgeous Modernista creation of architect Puig I Cadafalch

bottles, dating from predynastic Egypt to modern times, which you can look at but unfortunately not sniff.

### 🅞 MUSEU EGIPCI

☎ 93 488 01 88; www.museuegipci .com; Carrer de València 284; adult/senior & student €7/5; ⌚ 10am-8pm Mon-Sat, to 2pm Sun; Ⓜ Passeig de Gràcia
This oddball private collection features more than 700 exhibits, including ceramics, mummies, friezes, jewellery, masks and statuettes from ancient Egypt.

### 🅞 PALAU DEL BARÓ QUADRAS

☎ 93 238 73 37; www.casaasia.es; Avinguda Diagonal 373; ⌚ 10am-8pm Mon-Sat, to 2pm Sun; Ⓜ Diagonal

Remodelled by Puig i Cadafalch between 1902 and 1904, this palace houses the Casa Asia cultural centre. It has fine stained glass and its facade is ornamented with detailed, often rather zany, neo-Gothic carvings. Pop in for a cuppa at the cafe.

### 🅞 PALAU MONTANER

☎ 93 317 76 52; Carrer de Mallorca 278; adult/child & senior €5/2.50; ⌚ guided visits 10.30am (English), 11.30am (Catalan) & 12.30pm (Spanish) Sat, 10.30am (Catalan), 11.30am (Spanish) & 12.30pm (Catalan) Sun; Ⓜ Passeig de Gràcia
Interesting on the outside and made all the more enticing by its gardens, this creation by Domènech i Montaner is spectacular on the inside. Completed in 1896, its central feature is a

grand staircase beneath a broad, ornamental skylight. The interior is laden with sculptures, mosaics and fine woodwork.

### ☑ UNIVERSITAT DE BARCELONA

☎ 93 402 11 00; www.ub.edu; Gran Via de les Corts Catalanes 585; ☼ 9am-9pm Mon-Fri; Ⓜ Universitat

The city's venerable university, a glorious mix of Romanesque, Gothic, Islamic and Mudéjar, is an eclectic caprice of the 19th century. Wander into the main hall, up the grand staircase and around the various leafy cloisters. The richly decorated main auditorium upstairs is the Paranimfo. Take a stroll in the gardens out back.

## 🛍 SHOP

Shoppers may never extricate themselves from l'Eixample. Big-name brands line Passeig de Gràcia and La Rambla de Catalunya, but the nearby streets crawl with curious little boutiques purveying everything imaginable.

### 🛍 ADOLFO DOMÍNGUEZ
*Fashion*

☎ 93 487 41 70; www.adolfodominguez .com; Passeig de Gràcia 32; Ⓜ Passeig de Gràcia

This Galician chain is one of Spain's most celebrated fashion stores. Designs are classic and a little conservative, but all in time-less good taste for men, women and kids, with exquisite tailoring and quality materials. This branch is enormous.

### 🛍 ALTAÏR *Books*

☎ 93 342 71 71; www.altair.es; Gran Via de les Corts Catalanes 616; Ⓜ Universitat

If you need any encouragement in planning your next trip, this travel specialist will give you a nudge in the right direction. The range of local-interest books, guides to everywhere and maps

### SHOPPING & SNACKING ON LA RAMBLA DE CATALUNYA

The city tourist board touts the shopping wonders of Passeig de Gràcia, but a wander along La Rambla de Catalunya (D4) is another experience, especially during the warmer months when bars and restaurants put tables out on the broad, tree-lined pedestrian strip. Starting from the southeast, pop in and out of Mayol (No 27, shoes), Pilar Burgos (No 32, shoes), Muxart (No 47, accessories), Zara (No 67, fashion), Furla (No 77, bags), Turkestan (No 76, rugs), Conti (No 78, various top fashion labels), Perfumería Júlia (No 97, perfumes), Aramis (No 103, classic fashion) and a whole lot more. Don't miss the pastries in Mauri (p122). Stop for a coffee, beer or meal on the way and contemplate the decor of the many magnificent facades.

is impressive. And there's a travel agency downstairs.

## 🛍 ANTONIO MIRÓ
*Fashion*

☎ 93 487 06 70; www.antoniomiro.es in Spanish; Carrer del Consell de Cent 349; Ⓜ Passeig de Gràcia

The doyen of Barcelona couture, Antonio Miró made his name by producing elegant and unpretentious classic fashion of the highest quality for men and women – anything from ball gowns to T-shirts. Miró also does an attractive line in accessories.

## 🛍 ARMAND BASI
*Fashion*

☎ 93 215 14 21; www.armandbasi .com; Passeig de Gràcia 49; Ⓜ Passeig de Gràcia

Once the outfitter of James Bond and now focusing on design, Armand Basi is a stylish stalwart who does slinky numbers for the gals, uptown suits in black, evening wear, leather jackets and accessories.

## 🛍 BAGUÉS
*Jewellery*

☎ 93 216 01 73; www.bagues.com; Passeig de Gràcia 41; Ⓜ Passeig de Gràcia

This is more than just any old jewellery store. The boys from Bagués have been chipping away at precious stones and moulding

metal since the 19th century, and many of their classic pieces have a flighty Modernista influence.

## 🛍 CAMPER *Shoes*

☎ 93 215 63 90; www.camper.com; Carrer de València 249; Ⓜ Passeig de Gràcia

This classic Mallorcan shoe merchant continues to stamp all over the international market by successfully treading the fine line between rebellion and commercialism. There are branches all over town.

## 🛍 CASA DEL LLIBRE *Books*

☎ 902 026407; www.casadellibro .com in Spanish; Passeig de Gràcia 62; ⏲ 9.30am-9.30pm Mon-Sat; Ⓜ Passeig de Gràcia

This chain of general bookstores is among the best-stocked in town. The 'home of the book' covers a broad range of subjects and has decent sections devoted to literature in English, French and other languages. It also organises readings and book presentations.

## 🛍 EL BULEVARD DELS ANTIQUARIS *Antiques*

☎ 93 215 44 99; www.bulevardels antiquaris.com; Passeig de Gràcia 55; Ⓜ Passeig de Gràcia

Part of the Bulevard Rosa shopping arcade, this stretch is crammed with more than 70 antique shops tempting you with the this-and-thats of times gone by. A few of the specialist shops to look out for include Brahuer (jewellery), Govary's (porcelain dolls) and Victory (crystal).

### 🛒 EL BULEVARD ROSA
*Shopping Arcade*
☎ 93 215 83 31; www.bulevardrosa
.com; Passeig de Gràcia 55-57;
Ⓜ Passeig de Gràcia

With more than 100 shops featuring some of the most interesting local designers of fashion and jewellery, this 1980s creation is the best mall in the city for style and a few hours of boutique-browsing.

### 🛒 EL CORTE INGLÉS
*Department Store*
☎ 93 306 38 00; www.elcorteingles
.es in Spanish; Plaça de Catalunya 14;
Ⓜ Catalunya

This monster of retail has everything you could possibly want and lots more that won't have crossed your mind. There's also a rooftop cafe with a splendid view. There are several branches across town.

### 🛒 ELS ENCANTS VELLS
*Market*
☎ 93 246 30 30; www.encantsbcn.com in Catalan; Plaça de les Glòries Catalanes; ⏲ 7am-6.45pm Mon, Wed, Fri & Sat; Ⓜ Glòries

Barcelona's most authentic flea market is 'the Old Charms', where bargain-hunters riffle through everything from battered old shoes and bric-a-brac to antique furniture and new clothes. A lot of it is junk, but it depends on what the stall holders have got their hands on the day you turn up. Go in the morning for the best choice.

### 🛒 FARRUTX
*Shoes*
☎ 93 215 06 85; www.farrutx.com; Carrer de Rosselló 218; Ⓜ Diagonal

Mallorca's Farrutx is one of the country's top shoemakers. It has been expertly dressing the heels of Barcelona's uptown women for decades, does a nice line in luxury sport shoes and tops it off with bags and other leather accessories.

### A FINE EIXAMPLE
Ildefons Cerdà conceived the gridlike Eixample (Extension) into which Barcelona grew from the late 19th century. However, developers disregarded the more utopian features of Cerdà's plan, which called for building on only two sides of each block and the provision of gardens within. Now, nearly 150 years later, the city has reclaimed some of these public spaces. The garden (and toddlers' pool in summer) around the **Torre de les Aïgues** (E4; Carrer de Roger de Llúria 56) water tower offers an insight into what could have been. More such spaces (sans pool) are being opened up all the time.

The quaint shop front of Joan Murrià

### FLORISTERÍA NAVARRO
*Florist*

☎ 93 457 40 99; www.floresnavarro
.com; Carrer de València 320; ⏰ 24hr;
Ⓜ Girona

Just met the love of your life? At
4am? Never fear, say it with flowers.
This barnlike florist shop has flowers and plants for every conceiv-
able situation. And it never closes.

### JOAN MURRIÀ *Food & Drink*

☎ 93 215 57 89; Carrer de Roger de
Llúria 85; ⏰ 9am-2pm & 5-8.30pm
Tue-Fri, 10am-2pm & 5-8.30pm Sat;
Ⓜ Passeig de Gràcia

Classic inside and out, this superb
grocer-delicatessen has been run
by the same family since the early
1900s and continues to showcase
the culinary wonders of Catalonia,
Spain and beyond. Inspect the
eye-catching facade, featuring
original designs by Modernista
painter Ramón Casas.

### JOAQUÍN BERAO *Jewellery*

☎ 93 215 00 91; www.joaquinberao
.com; La Rambla de Catalunya 74;
Ⓜ Passeig de Gràcia

For something special, head to
this elegant store showcasing the
exquisite avant-garde creations

of one of Spain's most prestigious jewellery designers. He works predominantly in silver and gold, and with new and entirely original concepts each season.

### 🎁 JORDI LABANDA
*Fashion*

**☎ 93 496 14 03; Carrer de Rosselló 232; Ⓜ Diagonal**

Celebrated Barcelona-raised cartoonist Jordi Labanda does original women's clothes (skirts, tops, bikinis), in which he tones down his comic colours a little but remains playful in design. In all his work there is an element of biting social commentary, so these are thinking-women's clothes!

### 🎁 JOSEP FONT *Fashion*

**☎ 93 487 21 10; www.josepfont.com; Carrer de Provença 304; Ⓜ Diagonal**

---

### WINNING WAYS OF CATALAN WINES

Things have changed since Roman days, when wine from Catalonia was known throughout the empire as cheap and cheerful plonk. The Penedès region, about 40km southwest of Barcelona, is the biggest producer and best known for its bubbly, *cava* (Freixenet and Codorníu are household names around the world). Torres is the biggest label in still wines. Look out for wines with the El Priorat (strong, quality reds) and Raïmat (reds and whites) labels.

---

One of the leading women's fashion designers in Barcelona (with branches in Paris, Madrid and Bilbao), Font presents a line of daringly sleek and sexy items in no-nonsense colours. Peer inside this basement location for the beautiful tiles and minimalist decor alone.

### 🎁 LAIE *Books*

**☎ 93 318 17 39; www.laie.es in Spanish & Catalan; Carrer de Pau Claris 85; Ⓜ Urquinaona**

A leisure complex for the mind, this bookshop combines a broad range of books with a splendid **cafe** ( 🕑 9am-9pm Mon, to 1am Tue-Sat), an international outlook and accommodating staff.

### 🎁 LOEWE *Accessories*

**☎ 93 216 04 00; www.loewe.com; Passeig de Gràcia 35; Ⓜ Passeig de Gràcia**

Loewe is one of Spain's leading and oldest fashion stores, founded in 1846. It specialises in luxury leather (shoes, accessories and even travel bags). It also has lines in perfume, sunglasses, cufflinks, silk scarves and jewellery. This branch opened in 1943 in the Modernista Casa Lleó Morera.

### 🎁 MANGO *Fashion*

**☎ 93 215 75 30; www.mango.es; Passeig de Gràcia 21; Ⓜ Passeig de Gràcia**

Begun in Barcelona in the 1980s, Mango has gone massive around the world with its combination of

NEIGHBOURHOODS

L'EIXAMPLE

sexy and sassy couture, reliable fabrics and department-store prices.

### MARC 3 *Gifts, Art*
☎ 93 318 19 53; La Rambla de Catalunya 12; Ⓜ Catalunya

Step inside this cavern of posters, prints and original paintings. At the front end of the shop is a remarkably wide range of items depicting the city you're in. A cut above the standard in kitsch, they can make fine gifts.

### MAS BACUS *Food & Drink*
☎ 93 453 43 58; Carrer d'Enric Granados 68; ☽ 10am-10.30pm; ☒ FGC Provença

Bacus is the name and Bacchus is the game. One of several fine wine stores in this part of town, Mas Bacus is also a gourmet snack stop. It has a broad selection of local tipples and others of more distant provenance.

### NORMA COMICS *Comics*
☎ 93 244 84 23; www.normacomics .com in Spanish; Passeig de Sant Joan 7-9; Ⓜ Arc de Triomf

The largest comic store in the city (indeed the biggest comic-store chain in Europe) has a comic gallery and an astonishing international collection that stretches from *Batman* and *Tintin* through to Manga comics and more-or-less porn items such as *Kiss*. Kids will love all the comic hero toys, too.

### VINÇON *Homeware*
☎ 93 215 60 50; www.vincon.com; Passeig de Gràcia 96; Ⓜ Diagonal

Although it has a lofty reputation as the frame in which Spanish design evolves, this superb shop is relaxed and unpretentious. Pamper your aesthetic senses with a journey through its local and imported household wares. Wander upstairs and out onto the terrace for unusual sidelong views of La Pedrera (p110). The TincÇon (I'm Sleepy) annexe at Carrer de Rosselló 246 is in the same block and dedicated to the bedroom.

Visually varied Vinçon, design depot

# 🍴 EAT

Fine dining can be had all over l'Eixample, but you need to know where you're headed as there are few obvious concentrations. That said, you'll find more options on the southwest side of Passeig de Gràcia.

## 🍴 ALBA GRANADOS
*Mediterranean*                        €€

☎ 93 454 61 16; www.albagranados .com; Carrer d'Enric Granados 34; 🕑 lunch & dinner Mon-Sat; 🚇 FGC Provença; 🍽

In summer, try for one of two romantic tables for two on the 1st-floor balcony, truly unique in this town. Meat dishes are king here. The *carrillera de ternera* (a dark, soft meat from the neck of the cow) can be followed by exquisite desserts.

## 🍴 ALKÍMIA *Catalan*          €€

☎ 93 207 61 15; Carrer de l'Indústria 79; 🕑 lunch & dinner Mon-Fri; 🚇 Sagrada Família

Jordi Vila serves refined Catalan dishes with a twist in this white-walled restaurant a few blocks from La Sagrada Família. Seafood dominates the menu in this one-Michelin-star place. Go for a set menu of about a dozen small courses – foodies' heaven.

## 🍴 AMALTEA *Vegetarian*          €

☎ 93 454 86 13; www.restaurant amaltea.com; Carrer de la Diputació 164; 🕑 lunch Mon-Thu, lunch & dinner Fri & Sat; 🚇 Urgell; 🍽 🆅 ♿

The weekday set lunch (€10) offers a series of dishes that change frequently with the seasons. Savour an *escalopa de seitan* (seitan escalope) and *empanadillas* (pastry pockets stuffed with spinach and hiziki algae and tofu). At night, try the set two-course dinner menu (€14.50). The homemade desserts are tempting.

## 🍴 BODEGA LA SEPÚLVEDA
*Catalan*                        €€

☎ 93 323 59 44; Carrer de Sepúlveda 173bis; 🕑 lunch & dinner Mon-Sat; 🚇 Universitat; 🍽

The range of dishes in this classic Catalan eatery is a little overwhelming, mixing traditional choices (cold meats, cheeses and Catalan faves like *cap i pota,* a dish of chunks of fatty beef in gravy) with more surprising options like *carpaccio de calabacín con bacalao y parmesán* (thin zucchini slices draped in cod and parmesan cheese).

## 🍴 CAFÈ DEL CENTRE *Cafe*          €

☎ 93 488 11 01; Carrer de Girona 69; 🕑 8am-midnight Mon-Fri; 🚇 Girona

Step a century back into history in this cafe, in business since 1873. A

**Matthew Tree**
*Writer*

**How does a Londoner wind up writing novels in Catalan?** I came to Catalonia in 1978 and returned to live in 1984. My writing in English wasn't going well and an editor suggested I try in Catalan. From the first sentence it was like having struck gold! **Has Barcelona changed much?** In the 1970s there was tension as people started using Catalan again after 38 years of repression. Now it's normal to see people interchanging in Catalan. **Anything else?** In the 1980s, if you saw a tourist in Barcelona, people pointed. I remember seeing a few walking down Passeig de Gràcia in bikinis. **Now there's seven million a year. Too many?** It can be irritating in some bars having to ask for something five times in Catalan before staff stop speaking broken English! **Speaking of bars...** A favourite is Cafè del Centre (p119).

timber-top bar extends down the right side as you enter, fronted by a slew of marble-topped tables and dark timber chairs. Out back is an old piano. It exudes an almost melancholy air but gets busy at night.

### 🍴 CASA ALFONSO
*Mediterranean*　　　　　€

☎ 93 451 39 46; www.casaalfonso.com; Carrer de Roger de Llúria 6; ⏰ 9am-1am Mon-Sat; Ⓜ Urquinaona

In business since 1934, Casa Alfonso is perfect for a tapas stop at the long marble bar. Timber-panelled and festooned with old photos, posters and swinging hams, it attracts a faithful local clientele for its *flautas* (thin custom-made baguettes with your choice of filling), hams, cheeses, hot dishes and homemade desserts.

### 🍴 CASA CALVET
*Mediterranean*　　　　　€€€

☎ 93 412 40 12; www.casacalvet.es; Carrer de Casp 48; ⏰ lunch & dinner Mon-Sat; Ⓜ Urquinaona; ✕

Set on the ground floor of a Gaudí apartment block (see p108), this sophisticated restaurant is patronised by VIPs from far and wide, drawn by creative Mediterranean cooking with a Catalan bent. Savour Gaudí's genius as you enjoy your foie gras or ravioli stuffed with oysters.

### 🍴 CASA DARÍO
*Seafood*　　　　　€€

☎ 93 453 31 35; www.casadario.com in Spanish; Carrer del Consell de Cent 256; ⏰ lunch & dinner Mon-Sat, closed Aug; Ⓜ Universitat; ✕

This traditional Galician restaurant serves up a cornucopia of gifts of the sea. White-jacketed waiters waft around with platters overflowing with scallops, octopus, crab and lobster, to name a few.

### 🍴 CATA 1.81 *Tapas*　　€€
☎ 93 323 68 18; www.cata181.com; Carrer de València 181; ⏰ dinner Mon-Sat, closed Aug; Ⓡ FGC Provença

Treat yourself to a series of dainty gourmet dishes, such as *raviolis amb bacallà* (salt-cod dumplings) or *truita amb tòfona* (thick potato tortilla with a delicate trace of truffle). Since wines feature so prominently here, let rip with the list of fine Spanish tipples. A good option is one of the various tasting menus.

### 🍴 CERVESERIA CATALANA
*Tapas*　　　　　€€

☎ 93 216 03 68; Carrer de Mallorca 236; ⏰ lunch & dinner; Ⓜ Passeig de Gràcia; ✕

Come for coffee and croissants in the morning, or wait until lunch to choose from the profusion of tapas and *montaditos* (canapés). You can sit at the bar, on the pavement terrace or in the restaurant at the back. The variety of hot tapas, delectable salads and other snacks draws a well-dressed crowd (and we mean crowd) from all over the *barri*.

### ⊞ INOPIA *Tapas* €€–€€€
☎ 93 424 52 31; www.barinopia.com in Spanish; Carrer de Tamarit 104; dinner Tue-Fri, lunch & dinner Sat; M Poble Sec; V

Albert Adrià, brother of superchef Ferran, runs this bright, open, corner gourmet tapas bar to universal hurrahs. The featherweight tempura vegetables team up nicely with the chicken skewers. Getting a seat or spot at the bar can be a matter of patience.

### ⊞ MAURI *Cafe, Pastries* €
☎ 93 215 10 20; La Rambla de Catalunya 102; 8am-9pm Mon-Sat, to 3pm Sun; M Diagonal

Join the ladies who lunch for exquisite pastries, light snacks and piped music. The plush interior is capped by an ornately painted fresco at the entrance, which dates back to Mauri's first days in 1929. This is the kind of place that your mum would love.

### ⊞ PATAGONIA *Argentine* €€
☎ 93 304 37 35; Gran Via de les Corts Catalanes 660; lunch & dinner Mon-Sat; M Passeig de Gràcia

Argentine means beef in all its cuts and forms, and lots of it. You could ease your way in with empanadas, tiny pasty-type pies filled with, well, meat. Meat mains (you might want to skip the offal options) come with one of five side dishes. Try classics like *bife de chorizo* (sirloin) or Brazilian *picanha* (rump).

### ⊞ RESTAURANT ME *Asian* €€
☎ 93 419 49 33; Carrer de París 162; dinner Mon-Sat; M Hospital Clínic; ✕

The Vietnamese American chef whips up superb Asian dishes. The *curry vietnamita* is a symphony of seafood critters with noodles in a green curry, while the *confit de pato a las siete especias* is a succulent, vacuum-cooked thigh of duck with bok choy and orange.

### ⊞ SAÜC *Catalan* €€€
☎ 93 321 01 89; www.saucrestaurant .com; Passatge de Lluís Pellicer 12; lunch & dinner Tue-Sat; M Hospital Clínic; ✕

This basement spot is worth going the extra mile for. Decor is neutral, allowing diners to concentrate on each mouth-watering course of creative Catalan cooking presented in the €68 tasting menu (appetiser, five courses, cheese selection and two desserts).

## PUSHING THE BOAT OUT ON CARRER D'ARIBAU

From Thursday to Saturday nights the upper half of Carrer d'Aribau (B4) is transformed by the arrival of revellers from across town. Between Carrer de València and Avinguda Diagonal, the range of bars is astonishing. From white-jacketed-waiter cocktail bars to singalong dens, from Colombian dance spots to a Milan-style *aperitivo* joint, the place heaves. Later at night, a phalanx of bars, clubs and ill-disguised girlie bars along the continuation of this street above Avinguda Diagonal bumps and grinds until dawn.

### 🍽 SENSE PRESSA
*Spanish* €€-€€€

☎ 93 218 15 44; Carrer d'Enric Granados 96; 🕐 lunch & dinner Tue-Sat, lunch Mon; Ⓜ Diagonal

The name may mean 'not in a rush', but you'll need to hurry to book one of the handful of burgundy-linen-draped tables in this basement treasury of Spanish cookery. There's a wide range of meat and fish options, depending on the season and chef's whim. Push the boat out for a *suquet de llamantiol amb mongetes grosses* (lobster and bean stew).

### 🍽 TAKTIKA BERRI
*Basque, Tapas* €€

☎ 93 453 47 59; Carrer de València 169; 🕐 lunch & dinner Mon-Fri, lunch Sat; Ⓜ Hospital Clínic

Deep in the grid maze of l'Eixample is this Basque redoubt. You have two choices: hang around the bar (just try at the lunch rush hour!) and nibble away at the Basque-style tapas – the trick is to grab them from the

waitress as she transports them from the kitchen to the bar – or head out the back for a slap-up, sit-down meal.

### 🍽 TAPAÇ 24 *Tapas* €€

☎ 93 488 09 77; www.carlesabellan .com; Carrer de la Diputació 269; 🕐 8am-midnight; Ⓜ Passeig de Gràcia

Carles Abellán, master of Comerç 24 in La Ribera (p85), runs this delightful basement tapas haven, turning out gourmet versions of old faves. Specials include the *bikini* (usually a toasted ham and-cheese sandwich, but here the ham is cured and the truffle makes all the difference!) and a thick *arròs negre de sípia* (squid-ink black rice).

### 🍽 THAI GARDENS *Thai* €€

☎ 93 487 98 98; Carrer de la Diputació 273; 🕐 lunch & dinner Mon-Sat; Ⓜ Passeig de Gràcia; Ⓥ

One of the first and still one of the most authentic Thai experiences in town. The tall interior is filled with greenery and tables vary from intimate spots for two to big round affairs for festive groups. Take a nibble at a bit of everything with the set meal (€29).

# Y DRINK

## Y BAR MOODERN Bar

☎ 93 445 40 00; Carrer de Rosselló 265; 🕒 8am-2am Sun-Thu, to 3am Fri & Sat; Ⓜ Diagonal

Locals and guests mix in a sensual synergy in this uptown posers' bar, which is highly agreeable if you feel like a little London- or New York–style attitude in the hip setting of designer Hotel Omm. Just watching some of the less fiscally challenged cavort makes it worthwhile. When this sprawling foyer bar winds up, many folks head downstairs to the hotel's rather small Ommsession dance club.

## Y DIETRICH GAY TEATRO CAFÉ Cabaret

☎ 93 451 77 07; Carrer del Consell de Cent 255; 🕒 10.30pm-3am; Ⓜ Universitat

A classic of the Gaixample, this place hosts some of the best drag in the city in its elegant quarters – all timber finishings on two levels. Quiet during the week, it goes a little wild with drag shows, acrobats and dancing from Friday on.

## Y DISTRITO DIAGONAL Bar-Club

☎ 607 113602; www.distritodiagonal .com; Avinguda Diagonal 442; admission after 4am €15; 🕒 11pm-8.30am Fri & Sat; Ⓜ Diagonal

It's long and narrow, with a wee, elevated dance floor at the back. What makes the place is the weekend opening hours. And before 4am, it's free. You can drink quietly enough at the bar or shake your thing until breakfast time.

## Y DRY MARTINI Cocktail Bar

☎ 93 217 50 72; Carrer d'Aribau 162-166; 🕒 1pm-2am Sun-Thu, to 3am Fri & Sat; Ⓡ FGC Provença

For decades this has been one of the city's great cocktail joints, a

## GETTING LOOSE IN THE GAIXAMPLE

Gay bars and clubs are sprinkled across the city but especially concentrated in a small area of l'Eixample. Starting at the corner of Carrer de Balmes and Carrer del Consell de Cent (C5), move southwest along the latter, past the straight-friendly Hotel Axel, with its stunning rooftop bar in summer or basement drinking den, Underground. You'll soon start running into bars, especially around Carrer de Muntaner (C5), Carrer de Casanova (C5) and Carrer de Villarroel (C6). If in doubt, just follow the crowds of beautiful boys cruising arm-in-arm on weekend evenings.

classic of discreet, white-jacketed waiters who will whip up a fine, well, dry martini, or any other cocktail fantasy. Sit at the bar or plunge into the bloated leather lounges. Out the back is the Speakeasy restaurant.

### ▼ LA CHAPELLE *Bar*
☎ 93 453 30 76; Carrer de Muntaner 67; ⏱ 6pm-2am Mon-Thu, to 3am Fri & Sat; Ⓜ Universitat
A typical, long, narrow Eixample bar with white tiled walls like a 1930s hospital. It's replete with religious 'decor' – a plethora of crucifixes and niches that far outdoes what you'd find in any other 'chapel'. This is a relaxed gay meeting place that welcomes all comers.

### ▼ LES GENS QUE J'AIME *Bar*
☎ 93 215 68 79; Carrer de València 286; ⏱ 6pm-2.30am Sun-Thu, to 3am Fri & Sat; Ⓜ Passeig de Gràcia
Incurably romantic, this basement bar combines candlelight and privacy with antique red-velvet sofas and dark-wood furniture and trims. It's the perfect place for a night of sweet nothings.

### ▼ MICHAEL COLLINS PUB *Pub*
☎ 93 459 19 64; Plaça de la Sagrada Família 4; ⏱ noon-2am Sun-Thu, to 3am Fri & Sat; Ⓜ Sagrada Família
Of all the many Irish pubs in Barcelona, this is one of the most agree-

able. The Guinness is good and the punters, although many are foreigners, are generally residents rather than stag-night blow-ins.

### ▼ SWEET CAFÉ *Bar*
http://sweetcafebcn.blogspot.com in Spanish; Carrer de Casanova 75; ⏱ 8pm-3am Wed-Sun; Ⓜ Urgell
This illuminated red tunnel of a bar is an eclectic drinking choice. Gay-friendly but by no means exclusive, it attracts a broad spectrum of punters, some in search of the occasional live band or art expos.

## ★ PLAY
### ★ ANTILLA BCN *Club*
☎ 93 451 45 64; www.antillasalsa.com in Spanish; Carrer d'Aragó 141; ⏱ 11pm-6am; Ⓜ Urgell
*The* salsateca in town, this is the place to come for Cuban *son*, merengue, salsa and a whole lot more. If you don't know how to dance any of this, you may feel a little silly (as a bloke) but will probably get free lessons (if you're a lass). Blokes can come back at another time and pay for lessons.

### ★ ARENA MADRE *Club*
☎ 93 487 83 42; www.arenadisco.com; Carrer de Balmes 32; admission €6-12; ⏱ 12.30-6am; Ⓜ Passeig de Gràcia
Popular with a young gay crowd, Arena is one of the top clubs in

NEIGHBOURHOODS

L'EIXAMPLE

town for boys seeking boys. Keep an eye out for striptease nights on Monday, drag shows on Wednesday, and a combination of disco and Latin music to get those butts moving. Heteros are welcome but a minority. There are three other Arena clubs nearby.

### ⭐ DBOY Club
**www.dboyclub.com; Ronda de Sant Pere 19-21;** 🕑 **midnight-6am Fri-Sun & holidays;** Ⓜ **Urquinaona**
Once known as Salvation and a key club on the gay circuit, it has been given a complete overhaul (as well as a new name), with stunning lighting. Electronic music dominates the dance nights here. The Sunday night La Madame sessions are highly popular.

### ⭐ L'AUDITORI Classical Music
☎ **93 247 93 00; www.auditori.org; Carrer de Lepant 150; admission €17-65;** 🕑 **box office noon-9pm Mon-Sat;** Ⓜ **Monumental**
The permanent home of Barcelona's symphony orchestra (OBC) is a somewhat ugly venue for serious music lovers, designed by Rafael Moneo. Its comfortable (and acoustically unrivalled) main auditorium hosts orchestral performances, as well as occasional world-music jams. Chamber music is performed in a small, cosier and acoustically fabulous auditorium.

### ⭐ MASAJES A 1000 *Massage*
☎ **93 215 85 85; www.masajesa1000 .net in Spanish; Carrer de Mallorca 233; massages from €4 for 5min;** 🕑 **7am-1am;** 🚇 **FGC Provença**
Sightseeing, eating, drinking and all that traffic noise can become a bit much. For a quick restorative massage, pop by here. A voucher system operates – the more vouchers you buy, the greater your options for longer and more specific massage treatment.

### ⭐ METRO *Club*
☎ **93 323 52 27; www.metrodiscobcn .com; Carrer de Sepúlveda 185;** 🕑 **midnight-5am Sun-Thu, to 6am Fri & Sat;** Ⓜ **Universitat**
Both dance floors here are absolutely heaving at weekends (and on weekday theme nights), when a 90% gay crowd thumps to top-of-the-range house and techno. During the week it's dance-club pop and handbags ahoy, with strip nights, bingo events and other diversions, if you need any.

### ⭐ RENOIR FLORIDABLANCA *Cinema*
☎ **93 426 33 37; www.cinesrenoir.com in Spanish; Carrer de Floridablanca 135;** Ⓜ **Sant Antoni**
This cinema, handy for the nearby El Raval area, is one of the city's better locations for movies (main-

stream and off the wall) in the original language.

## ⭐ TEATRE NACIONAL DE CATALUNYA *Theatre*
☎ 93 306 57 00; www.tnc.es; Plaça de les Arts 1; admission €12-32; 🕑 box office 3-8pm Tue-Sat & 1hr before show; Ⓜ Glòries or Monumental

This hi-tech, classical-looking temple to Catalan theatre was designed by Ricard Bofill. It offers a broad range of theatre (mostly in Catalan), contemporary dance and a mixed bag of international performances.

## ⭐ ZAC CLUB *Live Music*
☎ 657 918555; www.zac-club.com in Spanish; Avinguda Diagonal 477; admission €12-15; 🕑 9pm-6am Thu-Sat; Ⓜ Hospital Clínic

A broad range of concerts is staged here most nights of the week. The small stage is occupied from 9pm to about midnight, from which point on the place converts to a small, rather congenial club.

# >GRÀCIA & PARK GÜELL

Gràcia was a separate village until 1897, when it was definitively annexed to an expanding Barcelona. If only because of its tight, narrow lanes and endless interlocking squares, it has maintained a unique and separate identity.

Fashionable among bohemians in the 1960s and '70s, it has since been somewhat gentrified. Judging by the tribes of students and other young folk that fill the countless bars by night, the process of heading upscale has had more of an effect on housing prices than on the district's inhabitants, who remain an eclectic bunch, far from the high-class, big-spending snobbery more associated with La Zona Alta.

There are few sights in Gràcia but the streets invite full immersion. The nooks and crannies, with everything from sushi bars to badly lit old taverns, are a source of endless fascination. The district goes a trifle mad in summer for the Festa Major de Gràcia (p31), which goes on for days around 15 August and sees the *barri* (neighbourhood) turned into one big party.

North of Gràcia lies one of Gaudí's extraordinary creations – the undulating Park Güell.

# GRÀCIA & PARK GÜELL

NEIGHBOURHOODS

GRÀCIA & PARK GÜELL

# ◉ SEE

## ◉ CASA MUSEU GAUDÍ

☎ 93 219 38 11; Park Güell, Carrer d'Olot 7; admission €4; ☾ 10am-8pm Apr-Sep, to 6pm Oct-Mar; Ⓜ Lesseps or Vallcarca or 🚌 24

Worth a gander if you're in Park Güell, this is the house where Gaudí spent many of his later years. The museum includes furniture designed by Gaudí and his mates, along with personal effects and an ascetically narrow bed upon which he probably

See how Gaudí lived at Casa Museu Gaudí

fantasised about completing La Sagrada Família.

## ◉ CASA VICENÇ

Carrer de les Carolines 22; Ⓜ Fontana
The turreted and vaguely Mudéjar-inspired 1888 Casa Vicenç was one of Gaudí's first commissions. This private house (which cannot be visited) is awash with ceramic colour and shape.

## ◉ MERCAT DE LA LLIBERTAT

☎ 93 415 90 93; Plaça de la Llibertat; ☾ 5-8pm Mon, 8am-2pm & 5-8pm Tue-Fri, 7am-3pm Sat; 🚇 FGC Gràcia

Built in the 1870s and covered over in 1893 in fizzy Modernista style, employing generous whirls of wrought iron, this market is emblematic of the Gràcia district, full of life and all kinds of fresh produce. The man behind it was Francesc Berenguer i Mestres (1866–1914), Gaudí's long-time assistant.

## ◉ PARK GÜELL

☎ 93 413 24 00; Carrer d'Olot 7; ☾ 10am-9pm Jun-Sep, to 8pm Apr, May & Oct, to 7pm Mar & Nov, to 6pm Dec-Feb; Ⓜ Lesseps or Vallcarca or 🚌 24

Gaudí's fantasy public park was meant to be a glorious gated playground for Barcelona's rich, but that idea didn't come off (see p22). Instead, the town hall bought it in 1922 and opened it to

## FORMULA FOR ADRENALINE

The motor-racing circuit at Montmeló, 20km northeast of the city, hosts the Spanish Grand Prix in late April or early May. Contact the **Circuit de Catalunya** ( ☎ 93 571 97 71; www .circuitcat.com; Carrer de Parets del Vallès, Montmeló) for details. Tickets cost €123 to €483. Purchase over the phone, at the track, online with **ServiCaixa** ( ☎ 902 332211; www .servicaixa.com) or at advance-sales desks in El Corte Inglés department stores. You can get a regular *rodalies* (local) train to Montmeló (€1.40, 30 minutes) but will need to walk about 3km or find a local taxi (about €10) to reach the track. On race days the **Sagalés bus company** ( ☎ 902 130014) often puts on buses from Passeig de Sant Joan (Map pp106–7, E3), between Carrer de la Diputació and Carrer del Consell de Cent.

the common folk. Just inside the main entrance on Carrer d'Olot (immediately recognisable by the two *Hansel and Gretel* gatehouses), visit the park's **Centre d'Interpretació** ( ☎ 93 285 68 99; adult/under 16yr/student €2.30/free/1.80; ⏲ 11am-3pm) in the Pavelló de Consergeria, the curvaceous, Gaudian former porter's home, which hosts a display on Gaudí's building methods and park history.

## 🖼 SHOP

**🖼 RED MARKET** *Fashion*
☎ 93 218 63 33; Carrer de Verdi 20;
⏲ 5-9.30pm Mon, 11.30am-2pm & 5-9.30pm Tue-Sat; Ⓜ Fontana
Carrer de Verdi is one of the most enticing streets in Gràcia. Home to everyone's favourite art-house cinema (p133), a colourful series of eclectic bars and restaurants, and practical things like internet centres, it also hosts numerous little fashion boutiques. This shop

is great for casual urban wear and accessories.

## 🍴 EAT

**🍴 BILBAO** *Spanish* €€
☎ 93 458 96 24; Carrer del Perill 33;
⏲ lunch & dinner Mon-Sat; Ⓜ Diagonal
You'll need to book for generous portions of hearty Spanish grub (the emphasis is on juicy meat). The dim lamps, dusty bottles along the rear wall and attentive service will make you want to linger in what seems, from the outside, no more than a scruffy neighbourhood bar.

**🍴 CAL BOTER** *Catalan* €€
☎ 93 458 84 62; Carrer de Tordera 62;
⏲ lunch & dinner Tue-Sun; Ⓜ Joanic
Catalan families in high spirits pile in here for piles of local grub, such as the curious *mar i muntanya* (surf and turf) combination of *bolets i gambes* (mushrooms and prawns). Stacks of meat and fish are on hand

and the atmosphere is of another, simpler age. A few tables are scattered in the leafy little backyard.

### 🍴 GOLIARD *Modern* €€

☎ 93 207 31 75; Carrer de Progrés 6; 🕐 lunch & dinner Mon-Fri, dinner Sat & Sun; Ⓜ Diagonal; Ⓥ

Goliard, tucked away down a back alley, is a haven of designer cooking at reasonable prices. Some of the salads are especially interesting, including anything from eel to calamari. You're likely to find kangaroo on the menu. Tables are jammed in a little close to one another but, overall, the place is homey.

### 🍴 SOL SOLER *Tapas* €

☎ 93 217 44 40; Plaça del Sol 21-22; 🕐 5pm-1.30am Mon, 3pm-2am Tue-Fri, 1pm-2.30am Sat, 1pm-2am Sun; Ⓜ Fontana; Ⓥ

On a corner of the Gràcia district's liveliest *plaça,* this busy tapas bar has faded bohemian chic, relaxed music, intimate lighting and marble-topped tables on which to enjoy a range of tasty fare – anything from couscous or lasagne to deep-fried chicken wings.

# 🍸 DRINK

### 🍸 BAR CANIGÒ *Bar*

☎ 93 213 30 49; Carrer de Verdi 2; 🕐 5pm-2am Mon-Thu, to 3am Fri & Sat; Ⓜ Fontana

Especially welcoming in winter, this corner bar on an animated square is a timeless spot to simply sip on an Estrella beer around rickety old marble-top tables and indulge in animated banter. There's also a pool table.

### 🍸 LA BAIGNOIRE *Wine Bar*

Carrer de Verdi 6; 🕐 4pm-3am; Ⓜ Fontana

Feel like sampling a series of different fine wines? This popular tiny wine bar is the answer. Grab a stool and high table and order national and a few foreign grape nectars by the glass (beer and cocktails available too).

### 🍸 MUSICAL MARIA *Bar*

Carrer de Maria 5; 🕐 9pm-3am; Ⓜ Diagonal

For a great rock 'n' roll atmosphere, step back in time to this Gràcia classic. Play pool at the back or elbow your way to the bar for a beer or cocktail. Musical nostalgia takes care of the rest in this cramped but agreeable little bar.

### 🍸 RAÏM *Tavern*

Carrer de Progrés 34; 🕐 1pm-2am; Ⓜ Diagonal

If you like your taverns unchanged since God knows when, with huge old wine barrels and a motley crew of punters, from local guzzlers through to grungy Erasmus students, this place could be for you. Judging by the wall-to-wall photos of Cuba, the owners have quite an affection for the island. The mojitos are excellent.

### ⍟ SABOR A CUBA *Bar*
☎ 600 262003; Carrer de Francisco Giner 32; ☽ 10pm-2.30am Mon-Thu, to 3am Fri & Sat; Ⓜ Diagonal

Ruled since 1992 by the charismatic Havana-born Angelito is this home of *ron y son* (rum and sound). Cubans and Cuba fans sip mojitos and shake their stuff in

this diminutive, good-humoured hang-out.

## ⭐ PLAY
### ⭐ VERDI *Cinema*
☎ 93 238 79 90; www.cines-verdi .com; Carrer de Verdi 32; admission €5-7; Ⓜ Fontana

Verdi was the first Barcelona cinema to specialise in original-language movies. The location, surrounded by bars and restaurants, is an added incentive. It also runs **Verdi Park** (Carrer de Torrijos 49), in the next street over; there are nine screens between the two sites.

# >MONTJUÏC, SANTS & POBLE SEC

Overlooking the sea, Montjuïc hill is a cornucopia of activities. Locals escape here for a breath of fresh air. A series of pretty gardens could occupy much of a lazy day (see p16), but there is plenty to see, from the Castell de Montjuïc at the hill's apex to the Fundació Joan Miró and majestic Museu Nacional d'Art de Catalunya. Nearby are more museums, the Olympic stadium, pools, concert venues and the Poble Espanyol, a composite of Spanish towns in miniature.

A varied and growing collection of inviting eateries and bars lines the higgledy-piggledy streets of Poble Sec, which slopes down the northeast face of the hill towards Avinguda del Paral.lel. You can also visit a civil war air-raid shelter here.

To the northwest of Montjuïc sprawls the mostly working-class district of Sants, which also happens to be home to the city's main train station.

## MONTJUÏC, SANTS & POBLE SEC

Please see over for map

The heart of the original district of Sants, immediately southwest of the train station, is worth a wander if you want to see a part of older Barcelona without a single tourist in sight.

# ⊙ SEE

## ⊙ CAIXAFORUM

☎ 93 476 86 00; www.fundacio.lacaixa .es in Catalan & Spanish; Avinguda del Marquès de Comillas 6-8; admission free; ☺ 10am-8pm Tue-Fri & Sun, to 10pm Sat; Ⓜ Espanya

An outstanding brick caprice by Modernista architect Josep Puig i Cadafalch, this building has been transformed by the Caixa building society from factory and cavalry barracks into one of Barcelona's best art exhibition spaces. Two or three separate exhibitions are on at any one time.

## ⊙ CASTELL DE MONTJUÏC

☎ 93 329 86 13; adult/senior & student €3/1.50; ☺ 9.30am-8pm Tue-Sun late Mar-late Oct, 9.30am-5pm Tue-Fri, 9.30am-7pm Sat, Sun & holidays late Oct-late Mar; 🚍 PM or telefèric

An assortment of weapons, uniforms, armour, tin soldiers and instruments of war from down the centuries make up the somewhat sombre collection of the Museu Militar, housed in the 18th-century fortress that overlooks Barcelona. The view from the ramparts is magnificent but the future of the museum itself in doubt, as the city government has taken over the fort's management and vowed to dismantle a museum it views as politically quite incorrect.

## ⊙ FUNDACIÓ JOAN MIRÓ

☎ 93 443 94 70; http://fundaciomiro -bcn.org; Plaça de Neptu; adult/senior & child €8/6, temporary exhibitions €4/3; ☺ 10am-8pm (to 7pm Oct-May) Tue, Wed, Fri & Sat, to 9.30pm Thu, to 2.30pm Sun & holidays; 🚍 50, 55 or PM, or funicular

Joan Miró left his home town this art foundation, a homage to

Rooftop installations at Fundació Joan Miró

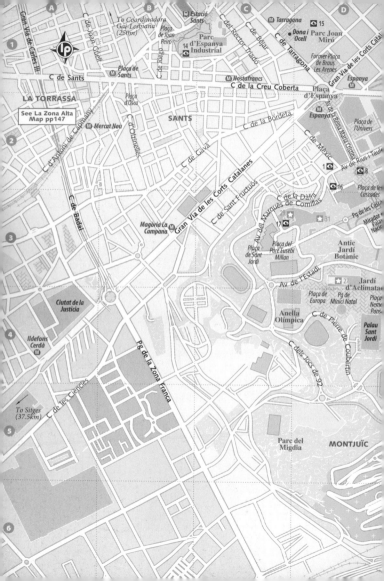

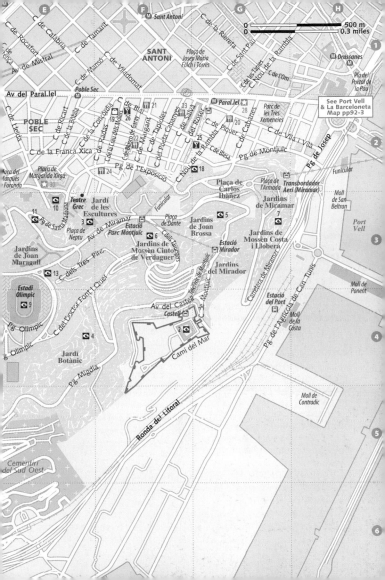

himself, in 1971. Its light-filled buildings are crammed full with a broad spectrum of Miró's work, from early sketches to giant, bold canvasses. The collection comprises around 300 paintings, 150 sculptures, some textiles and more than 7000 drawings spanning his entire life, although only a small portion is ever on display. At least one temporary exhibition on someone else is also usually held here at any given moment.

### GARDENS
🕙 10am–sunset; 🚌 50 or PM
The varied gardens and play areas of **Jardins de Joan Brossa** (Carrer de Montjuïc) spread out over what was once a funfair. The beautiful, cool **Jardins de Mossèn Cinto de Verdaguer** (Carrer dels Tarongers) are devoted to bulbs and aquatic plants, from tulips to water lilies. A longish wander downhill from the Castell de Montjuïc, the **Jardins de Mossèn Costa i Llobera** (Carretera de Miramar) are of particular interest for their collection of tropical and desert plants – including a forest of cacti. For more about Montjuïc's gardens see p16.

### JARDÍ BOTÀNIC
☎ 93 426 49 35; www.jardibotanic.bcn
.es; Carrer del Doctor Font i Quer 2;
adult/under 16yr/student €3.50/free/1.70,
last Sun of month free; 🕙 10am–8pm

> ### WATERWORKS IN THE ALTOGETHER
> You can get all your gear off year-round at the Piscines Bernat Picornell (p144), the Olympic pool on Montjuïc. On Saturday, between 9pm and 11pm, the pool (with access to sauna and steam bath) is open only to nudists (adult/child and senior €4.80/3.45). On Sunday from October to May the indoor pool is also for nudists only, from 4.15pm to 6pm.

Jun-Aug, to 7pm Apr, May & Sep, to 6pm Feb, Mar & Oct, to 5pm Nov-Jan; 🚌 50, 61 or PM
Concentrating on a 'Mediterranean' flora theme, this botanic garden features thousands of species that thrive in similar climates all over the world, from Spain to Turkey, Australia to South Africa and California to Chile.

### LA FONT MÀGICA
Avinguda de la Reina Maria Cristina;
🕙 every half-hour 7-8.30pm Fri & Sat Oct-late Jun, 9.30-11.30pm Thu-Sun late Jun-Sep; Ⓜ Espanya
Delightfully over the top, the biggest of Montjuïc's famous fountains splashes into life with an irresistible summer-evening extravaganza of music and light. Whether it's to the tune of Tchaikovsky or ABBA, you'll be mesmerised by the waterworks.

La Font Màgica – lights, music, fountain!

### 🔵 L'ANELLA OLÍMPICA & ESTADI OLÍMPIC

**Avinguda de l'Estadi; admission free;**
**🕐 10am-8pm Apr-Sep, to 6pm Oct-Mar;**
**🚌 50, 61 or PM**

One for sports fans. L'Anella Olímpica (Olympic Ring) is the group of installations built for the main events of the 1992 Olympics. They include the Estadi Olímpic, which is open to the public when Espanyol (the 'other' football team) isn't battling it out here.

### 🔵 MUSEU D'ARQUEOLOGIA DE CATALUNYA

**☎ 93 424 65 77; www.mac.es; Passeig de Santa Madrona 39-41; adult/child €3/2; 🕐 9.30am-7pm Tue-Sat, 10am-2.30pm Sun; 🚌 55 or PM**

This archaeology museum mainly features artefacts discovered in Catalonia and Mediterranean Spain, from copies of pre-Neanderthal skulls to jewel-studded Visigothic crosses. It also houses a statue of a splendidly endowed, and routinely aroused, Priapus (the god of male procreative power) that we're not allowed to inspect closely.

### 🔵 MUSEU ETNOLÒGIC

**☎ 93 424 64 02; www.museuetnologic .bcn.cat in Catalan; Passeig de Santa Madrona 16-22; adult/under 12yr/senior & student €3.50/free/1.75, 1st Sun of month free; 🕐 noon-8pm Tue-Sat, 11am-3pm Sun late Jun-late Sep, 10am-7pm Tue & Thu, 10am-2pm Wed & Fri-Sun late Sep-late Jun; 🚌 55**

The permanent exhibition, Ètnic, includes several thousand

## WORTH THE TRIP: GIRONA, FIGUERES & SITGES

If you want to taste life away from the big city, several easy and worthwhile one-day excursions suggest themselves.

Regular trains from Barcelona make a sluggish but rewarding day trip northeast to **Girona** (91km, or up to 1½ hours) possible. Huddled in multicoloured confusion on the banks of the Onyar, this medieval town is delightful. The majestic **cathedral** ( ☎ 972 21 44 26; www .catedraldegirona.org; Plaça de la Catedral; museum admission €4, Sun free; 🕑 10am-2pm & 4-7pm Tue-Sat Mar-Jun, 10am-8pm Tue-Sat Jul-Sep, 10am-2pm & 4-6pm Tue-Sat Oct-Feb, 10am-2pm Sun & holidays year-round), with its irregular Romanesque cloister and power-ful Gothic interior, lords it over the rest of the town. Study Girona's history at the **Museu d'Història de la Ciutat** ( ☎ 972 22 22 29; www.ajuntament.gi/museuciutat; Carrer de la Força 27; adult/senior & under 16yr/student €3/free/2; 🕑 10am-2pm & 5-7pm Tue-Sat, 10am-2pm Sun & holidays) and wander the narrow streets of the medieval Jewish district around Carrer de la Força. Cross the river for the engaging **Museu del Cinema** ( ☎ 972 41 27 77; www.museudelcinema.org; Carrer de Sèquia 1; adult, senior & student/under 16yr €4/free; 🕑 10am-8pm Tue-Sun May-Sep, 10am-6pm Tue-Fri, 10am-8pm Sat, 11am-3pm Sun Oct-Apr). You might just squeeze in a swift, early dinner, as the last train back down to Barcelona leaves around 9.20pm.

wide-ranging items on show in three themed sections: Orígens (Origins), Pobles (Peoples) and Mosaics. Along with lots of material from rural areas of Catalonia and other parts of Spain, the museum's collections include items from Australia, Japan and Morocco.

### 🅒 MUSEU NACIONAL D'ART DE CATALUNYA (MNAC)

☎ 93 622 03 76; www.mnac.es; Mirador del Palau Nacional; adult/senior & under 15yr/student €8.50/free/6, 1st Sun of month free; 🕑 10am-7pm Tue-Sat, to 2.30pm Sun & holidays; Ⓜ Espanya

The grandest and worthiest of all Barcelona's art museums, the MNAC gathers under one roof a plethora of Catalan works that range from the Middle Ages to well into the 1900s. The Roman-esque art in particular is a unique experience (see p14).

### 🅒 MUSEU OLÍMPIC I DE L'ESPORT

☎ 93 292 53 79; www.fundaciobarce lonaolimpica.es; Avinguda de l'Estadi s/n; adult/senior & child/student €4/free/2.50; 🕑 10am-8pm Wed-Mon Apr-Sep, to 6pm Wed-Mon Oct-Mar; 🚍 50, 61 or PM

Just over the road from the Olympic stadium, this sports museum is an interactive and visual smorgasbord of sporting

**Figueres**, 38km further north from Girona, has one star attraction: the **Teatre-Museu Dalí** ( ☎ 972 67 75 00; www.salvador-dali.org; Plaça de Gala i Salvador Dalí 5; adult/student €11/8; ☺ 9am-8pm Jul-Sep, 9.30am-6pm Mar-Jun & Oct, 10.30am-6pm Nov-Feb), a marvellously loopy museum (and mausoleum) that Salvador Dalí created in honour of himself. It's jammed with art and gizmos, making for a unique voyage into his distorted world. You could fill in a day here with a couple of other museums and sprawling fortress. In a hurry? Leave Barcelona early and take in the Teatre-Museu Dalí here and the old town of Girona in one (longish) day.

Only half an hour southwest of Barcelona by train, **Sitges** is a unique resort that in summer attracts hordes of fashionable city folk and a huge international gay set. A former fishing village, it was a trendy hang-out for artists and bohemians in the 1890s and has remained one of Spain's more unconventional resorts ever since. You won't have much company in winter, as you visit its three **museums** ( ☎ 93 894 03 64; adult/child/student combined ticket €6.40/free/3.50; ☺ 10am-2pm & 5-9pm Tue-Sun Jul-Sep, 10am-1.30pm & 3-6.30pm Tue-Fri, 10am-7pm Sat, 10am-3pm Sun Oct-Jun), admire the sun-bleached baroque church atop a bluff over the beach, soak up the village atmosphere and wonder if it's too cold for a dip at the nude beach southwest of town.

For train timetables and prices from Barcelona to Girona, Figueres and Sitges, check out www.renfe.es.

history. It's centred on Olympic history but delves into anything from Formula 1 racing to the development of cricket under the British Raj.

### ☺ PARC D'ESPANYA INDUSTRIAL
**Carrer de Sant Antoni;** ☺ **10am-sunset;** Ⓜ **Sants Estació**
Maligned by many, this playfully postmodern park comprises what look like space-age watchtowers overlooking a boating lake and a dragon sculpture that's popular with kiddies. It's transformed when illuminated at night and worth a look if you're waiting for a train at Estació Sants.

### ☺ PARC JOAN MIRÓ
**Carrer de Tarragona;** Ⓜ **Tarragona**
The only reason for happening along to this park behind the former Les Arenes bullring (being converted into a leisure and shopping complex) is to admire Joan Miró's towering phallic sculpture, *Dona i Ocell* (Woman and Bird), in the park's western corner.

### ☺ PAVELLÓ MIES VAN DER ROHE
☎ **93 423 40 16; www.miesbcn.com; Avinguda del Marquès de Comillas s/n; adult/under 18yr/student €4/free/2;** ☺ **10am-8pm;** Ⓜ **Espanya**
This is a replica of a structure erected for – and demolished

Bronze reproduction of Alba (Dawn) by Georg Kolbe, in the Pavelló Mies van der Rohe (p141)

with – the 1929 World Exhibition. In hindsight it was considered a milestone of modern architecture and was rebuilt in 1986. With a light and airy design comprising horizontal planes, it reveals Mies van der Rohe's vision of a new urban environment.

### POBLE ESPANYOL

☎ 93 508 63 30; www.poble-espanyol .com; Avinguda del Marquès de Comillas; adult/child/senior & student €8/5/6; 🕙 9am-8pm Mon, to 2am Tue-Thu, to 4am Fri & Sat, to midnight Sun; M Espanya or 🚌 50, 61 or PM

Something of an impostor, the Spanish Village was put together for the 1929 World Exhibition. It comprises replicas of famous buildings and examples of traditional architecture from all over Spain. For a tourist trap, it's quite engaging.

### REFUGI 307

☎ 93 256 21 22; Carrer Nou de la Rambla 169; admission €3; 🕙 tours 11am-2pm Sat & Sun; M Paral.lel

Barcelona was the city most heavily bombed from the air during the Spanish civil war and was dotted with more than 1300 air-raid shelters. This one, open to the public, is a warren of low, narrow tunnels that was slowly extended as the war dragged on. The half-hour tours (in Catalan or Spanish; book ahead for English or French) explain how it worked.

# 🛍 SHOP

## 🛍 ELEPHANT *Books*

☎ 93 443 05 94; www.lfant.biz; Carrer de la Creu dels Molers 12; ⏰ 10am-8pm; Ⓜ Poble Sec

This bright bookshop is off the main tourist tracks but is a helpful haven of books in the Queen's English. Stock ranges from fiction to kids' stuff, with a smattering of reference works and a healthy secondhand section.

# 🍴 EAT

## 🍴 ELCHE *Catalan* €€

☎ 93 441 30 89; Carrer de Vila i Vilà 71; ⏰ lunch & dinner; Ⓜ Paral.lel; ♿

Some places are just good at what they do, and keep doing it. Hidden away from the busy old-town centre, this old-style restaurant has been serving up a variety of paellas, rice dishes and *fideuà* (similar to paella, but made with vermicelli noodles) since the 1960s.

## 🍴 LA BELLA NAPOLI *Italian* €-€€

☎ 93 442 50 56; Carrer de Margarit 12; ⏰ lunch Tue, lunch & dinner Wed-Sun; Ⓜ Poble Sec; ♿

Never will the Catalans seem so much the dour lot they are sometimes made out to be as when you descend into this isle of Neapolitan nuttiness. The staff are mostly from Naples or thereabouts, are full of teasing humour and bring you some of the best pizza in Barcelona.

## 🍴 LA TOMAQUERA *Spanish* €-€€

☎ 93 441 85 18; Carrer de Margarit 5; ⏰ lunch & dinner Tue-Sat; Ⓜ Poble Sec

It's first in, first seated in this knockabout eatery, where waiters move like rockets delivering dishes of hearty grub and carafes sloshing with wine. Try the house speciality of snails or the *cassola de cigales* (a crayfish hotpot for €17.75). It doesn't take credit cards.

## 🍴 QUIMET I QUIMET *Tapas* €-€€

☎ 93 442 31 42; Carrer del Poeta Cabanyes 25; ⏰ lunch & dinner Tue-Sat, lunch Sun; Ⓜ Paral.lel; ✗

This postage-stamp-sized tapas bar is a gourmet paradise in miniature. Let the bar staff combine a few canapés, seafood tapas, cream cheese or whatever is going.

## 🍴 XEMEI *Venetian* €€

☎ 93 553 51 40; Passeig de l'Exposició 85; ⏰ lunch & dinner Wed-Mon; Ⓜ Poble Sec; ✗

Xemei is a teeny slice of Venice on the side of Montjuïc hill. Such delicacies as *bigoi in salsa veneziana* (a thick spaghetti in an anchovy and onion sauce) or *paccheri* (a Neapolitan tubular pasta)

in a cuttlefish sauce are just two of the tempting pasta options.

# ▼ DRINK

## ▼ MAUMAU UNDERGROUND
*Bar-Club*
☎ 93 441 80 15; www.maumaunderground.com in Spanish; Carrer de la Fontrodona 33; 🕙 11pm-2.30am Thu, to 3am Fri & Sat; Ⓜ Paral.lel

Funk, soul, hip-hop – you never know what you might run into in this Poble Sec music and dance haunt. Above the backlit bar a huge screen spews forth psychedelic images; on Sunday afternoon it converts to a football screen for laid-back fans.

## ▼ TINTA ROJA *Bar*
☎ 93 443 32 43; Carrer de la Creu dels Molers 17; 🕙 8pm-1am Wed & Thu, 8pm-3am Fri & Sat, 7pm-midnight Sun; Ⓜ Poble Sec

Through a succession of tunnel-like spaces all suffused with reddish light, you penetrate to an area where anything could happen, from theatre to tango or acrobatics. The hushed atmosphere is always pleasant for a tipple.

# ⭐ PLAY

## ⭐ PISCINES BERNAT PICORNELL *Gym*
☎ 93 423 40 41; www.picornell.cat in Catalan; Avinguda de l'Estadi 30-38;

adult/senior & under 15yr/15-25yr €9.20/5.15/5.60, outdoor pool only Jun-Sep adult/6-14yr & senior €5.10/3.55; 🕙 6.45am-midnight Mon-Fri, 7am-9pm Sat, 7.30am-4pm Sun, outdoor pool 9am-9pm Mon-Sat, to 8pm Sun Jun-Sep, shorter hours rest of year; 🚌 50, 61 or PM; 👶

Included in the standard admission price to Barcelona's official Olympic pool is use of the gym, saunas and spa bath. There are also sessions for nudists – see the boxed text, p138.

## ⭐ SALA APOLO *Live Music, Club*
☎ 93 441 40 01; www.sala-apolo.com in Catalan & Spanish; Carrer Nou de la Rambla 113; 🕙 12.30-6am Wed-Sat, 10.30pm-3.30am Sun; Ⓜ Paral.lel

This former music hall is the scene of a fiery and eclectic dance and concert scene. Gigs (often starting about 9pm) range from world music to touring rock bands you'll never again see in a venue so cosy. After the encores, the hall is cleared for clubbing (a DJ team playing house, electro, neo-trance and more).

## ⭐ TABLAO DE CARMEN
*Flamenco*
☎ 93 325 68 95; www.tablaodecarmen.com; Carrer dels Arcs 9, Poble Espanyol; show only €35, with dinner €69-94; 🕙 shows 7.45pm & 10pm Tue-Sun; Ⓜ Espanya

Named after the great Barcelonin *bailaora* (flamenco dancer) Carmen Amaya, this place features a lively show with a full cast of guitarists, singers and dancers. Touristy, but not as bad as might be expected.

⭐ **TEATRE LLUIRE** *Theatre*
☎ 93 289 27 70; www.teatrelliure.com; Plaça Margarida Xirgu 1; admission €13-26; ⏱ box office 5-8pm; Ⓜ Espanya
With two spaces (Espai Lliure and Sala Fabià Puigserver), the Free Theatre hosts a variety of quality drama, almost exclusively in Catalan. There are occasional local international acts, including modern dance and music. A restaurant and bar makes a night out here easy.

⭐ **TERRRAZZA** *Club*
☎ 687 969825; www.laterrrazza.com in Spanish; Avinguda del Marquès de Comillas s/n; admission €18; ⏱ midnight-6am Fri & Sat May-Oct; Ⓜ Espanya
Some of the biggest international names play at this summertime must, which can be relied on for a range of the meatiest house, techno-trance and pop-rock on vinyl, and a clientele of extremely high-quality eye candy. Move to 'the terrace' for rejuvenation when you run out of steam.

# >LA ZONA ALTA

'The High Zone' is where most Barcelona folks with healthy bank accounts aspire to live, if possible in gated complexes or mansions with gardens (a rare luxury in Barcelona). To locals, the area really only refers to the hilly parts of town (such as Tibidabo) and districts like Sarrià, Sant Gervasi and Pedralbes. For ease of orientation we have pushed the border down to Avinguda Diagonal (where you can ferret out plenty of interesting nightlife and eating options) and let it overflow into Les Corts (to include the all-important FC Barcelona club's Camp Nou stadium).

Tibidabo is Barcelona's peak point (512m) and great for fresh air and views – on a good day you can see inland as far as Montserrat. The mountain, with its amusement park and rather bombastic church, is at the heart of the much wider Parc de Collserola, one of the city's few green lungs. Tibidabo gets its name from the devil, who, trying to tempt Christ, took him to a high place and said, in Latin: *'Haec omnia tibi dabo si cadens adoraberis me'* ('All this I will give you if you fall down and worship me').

Other highlights in La Zona Alta include the CosmoCaixa science museum and monuments of Pedralbes.

## LA ZONA ALTA

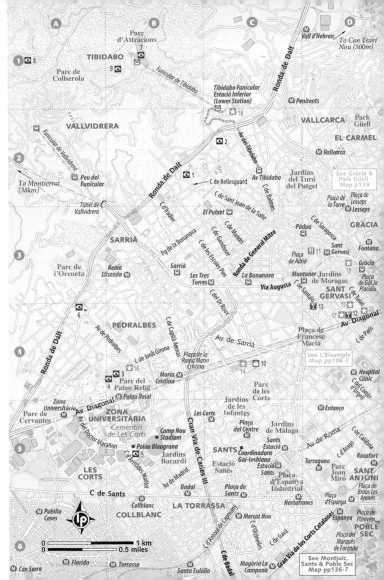

# 👁 SEE

## 📷 BELLESGUARD

**Carrer de Bellesguard;** 🚈 FGC Av Tibidabo

In typical Gaudí fashion, exposed brick, wrought iron and a sense of fairytale playfulness combine to give this private mansion, built in 1909, an unreal feel. It's a bit of a hike from the centre, so you need to be a fan of obscure Gaudiana well off any beaten track.

## 📷 COSMOCAIXA (MUSEU DE LA CIÈNCIA)

☎ 93 212 60 50; www.fundacio.lacaixa .es in Catalan & Spanish; Carrer de Teodor Roviralta 47-51; adult/student €3/2; 🕐 10am-8pm Tue-Sun; 🚌 60 or 🚈 FGC Av Tibidabo

Kids (and many grown-ups) can't help twiddling the knobs and engaging in experiments in this bright, playful science museum housed in a Modernista building (completed in 1909). The single greatest highlight is the re-creation over 1 sq km of a chunk of flooded Amazon rainforest (Bosc Inundat), complete with anacondas and tropical downpours. Elsewhere in the complex, everything from fossils to physics is touched on.

## 📷 MUSEU DE CERÀMICA

☎ 93 280 16 21; www.museuceramica .bcn.es; Palau Reial de Pedralbes,

Avinguda Diagonal 686; adult/student €4.20/2.40 (incl Museu de les Arts Decoratives), 1st Sun of month free; 🕐 10am-6pm Tue-Sat, to 3pm Sun & holidays; 🚇 Palau Reial

Welcome to perhaps the most fragile exhibition in Barcelona: an exceptional collection of Spanish ceramics dating from medieval times right up to the present day. The items on show include pieces by Miró and Picasso, as well as a charming selection of tiles depicting Catalan life.

## 📷 MUSEU DE LES ARTS DECORATIVES

☎ 93 280 16 21; www.museuartsdecora tives.bcn.es; Palau Reial de Pedralbes,

### FOLLOW THE BALLS

Passions run high in Barcelona over the fate of its star league football side, Football Club Barcelona (see p23). The team plays at the **Camp Nou stadium** (B5; ☎ 902 189900, from abroad 93 496 36 00; www.fcbarcelona.com; Carrer d'Arístides Maillol, Les Corts; tickets €14-170; 🕐 box office 9am-1.30pm & 3.30-6pm Mon-Fri; 🚇 Collblanc), and tickets for big matches can be hard to come by. Touts always work the stadium but you need to be careful, as security is tight. The same club boasts a champion basketball team. FC Barcelona shoots baskets at the **Palau Blaugrana** (B5), just by the main stadium. Tickets cost anything from €11 to €58, depending on the match and seat.

Avinguda Diagonal 686; adult/student €4.20/2.40 (incl Museu de Ceràmica), 1st Sun of month free; 10am-6pm Tue-Sat, to 3pm Sun & holidays; M Palau Reial Occupying the same former palace as the Museu de Ceràmica, this series of galleries overlooks a stunningly sumptuous oval throne room. It features a collection of furniture and decorative objects from the early Middle Ages to the kitsch 1970s.

### 🄲 MUSEU DEL FUTBOL CLUB DE BARCELONA

☎ 93 496 36 00; www.fcbarcelona.com; Carrer d'Aristides Maillol; adult/senior & child €8.50/6.80; ⏰ 10am-8pm Mon-Sat, to 2.30pm Sun & holidays mid-Apr–mid-Oct, 10am-6.30pm Mon-Sat, to 2.30pm Sun & holidays mid-Oct–mid-Apr; M Collblanc

The museum dedicated to one of the Europe's greatest football clubs

is a big draw. Among the quirkier paraphernalia are old sports board games, a 19th-century leather football, a life-sized diorama of a dressing room in the days of yore, posters and magazines from way back, and a *futbolín* (table soccer) collection. You can join a guided hour-long **tour** (adult/child €13/10.40; ⏰ until 1hr before museum closing time) of the stadium.

### 🄲 MUSEU-MONESTIR DE PEDRALBES

☎ 93 203 92 82; www.museuhistoria .bcn.cat; Baixada del Monestir 9; adult/ under 7yr/senior & student €6/free/4 (incl Museu d'Història de la Ciutat & Park Güell Centre d'Interpretació); ⏰ 10am-5pm Tue-Sat, to 3pm Sun Jun-Sep, 10am-2pm Tue-Sat, to 3pm Sun Oct-May; 🚆 FGC Reina Elisenda or 🚌 22 or 64 This peaceful museum pro- vides an absorbing insight into

The cloisters of Museu-Monestir de Pedralbes

medieval monastic life. The convent was founded in 1326 and is a jewel of Catalan Gothic with a three-storey cloister. The few remaining nuns have moved to nearby quarters. Around the cloister, visit the restored refectory, kitchen, stables, stores and infirmary. Built into the cloister walls are day cells where the nuns spent most of their time in prayer and devotional reading. Take the FGC train to Reina Elisenda, from where it's a short walk southwest. Buses 22 (from Plaça de Catalunya) and 64 (from La Barceloneta or along Carrer d'Aribau) also take you close.

### PARC D'ATRACCIONS
☎ 93 211 79 42; www.tibidabo.es; Plaça de Tibidabo 3-4; adult/child

Round and round it goes, where it stops, nobody knows — the Ferris wheel at Parc d'Atraccions under 1.2m €24/9; noon-10pm or 11pm Wed-Sun Jul-early Sep, shorter hours Sat, Sun & holidays rest of year; FGC Av Tibidabo, then Tramvia Blau & funicular

For the Ferris-wheel ride of your life – with the bonus of panoramic views from the top of Tibidabo – head for this cherished old-fashioned fun fair. It has all the usual thrills as well as the remarkable Museu d'Autòmats del Tibidabo, where you can see carnival games and gizmos from the 19th century. One of the scariest attractions is the Krueger Hotel: enter this house of horrors and be prepared to have your nerves rattled by ghouls and crims leaping out from the darkness. A new rollercoaster is planned for 2009. See also p27.

### PARC DE COLLSEROLA

93 280 35 52; www.parccollserola .net; Carretera de l'Església 92; FGC Peu de Funicular, then funicular to Baixador de Vallvidrera

Some 8000 hectares of parkland spread out in the hilly country southwest of Tibidabo, forming a marvellous escape hatch for city folk needing a little nearby nature. There are plenty of hiking and mountain-bike trails for those with nervous energy to expend. Pick up information at the **Centre d'Informació** ( 9.30am-3pm).

### TEMPLE DEL SAGRAT COR

93 417 56 86; Plaça de Tibidabo; 8am-7pm; FGC Av Tibidabo, then Tramvia Blau & funicular

The Church of the Sacred Heart is Barcelona's answer to Paris' Sacré Coeur. It's actually two churches, one on top of the other. The top one is surmounted by a giant statue of Christ and has a **lift** (€2; 10am-2pm & 3-6pm Mon-Sat, 10am-2pm & 3-7pm Sun) to take you to the roof for panoramic views.

### TORRE DE COLLSEROLA

93 211 79 42; www.torredecollserola .com; Carretera de Vallvidrera al Tibidabo; adult/child/senior €5/3/4; 11am-2.30pm & 3.30-6pm Wed-Sun Mar-Oct; FGC Peu de Funicular, then Funicular de Vallvidrera, then 111; P

Designed by Britain's Sir Norman Foster, this 288m telecommunications tower was built to bring the events of the 1992 Olympics to TV viewers around the world. A glass lift shoots up to an observation deck at 115m that affords splendid views of Tibidabo and the city.

# SHOP

### L'ILLA DEL DIAGONAL

*Shopping Centre*

93 444 00 00; www.lilla.com; Avinguda Diagonal 545; M Maria Cristina

This shopping centre, situated in the heart of the business district,

**NEIGHBOURHOODS**

**LA ZONA ALTA**

caters to uptowners and houses swanky designer stores and all the usual chains. In its heyday it was acclaimed for its architectural style.

# 🍴 EAT
## 🍴 CAN TRAVI NOU
*Catalan* €€
☎ 93 428 03 01; www.gruptravi.com; Carrer de Jorge Manrique s/n, Parc de la Vall d'Hebron; 🕐 lunch & dinner Mon-Sat, lunch Sun; Ⓜ Montbau; Ⓟ ✗

A rambling, 18th-century *masia* (farmhouse), with warm colours, a grandfather clock and a bucolic air, is a magical setting for a Catalan splurge. Several dining areas stretch out across two floors. The *arròs caldós amb llamàntol i cloïsses* (a rice stew with lobster and clams) is irresistible and they also do some tender grilled steaks.

## 🍴 EL RACÓ D'EN FREIXA
*Catalan* €€€
☎ 93 209 75 59; www.elracodenfreixa .com; Carrer de Sant Elies 22; 🕐 lunch & dinner Tue-Sat, closed Easter & Aug; 🚉 FGC Sant Gervasi

Ramon Freixa is one of the country's top chefs and is forever surprising diners in this hushed uptown residential hideaway. It's a coolly elegant place, with clean,

### WORTH THE TRIP: MONTSERRAT

Montserrat (Serrated Mountain) is the spiritual heart of Catalonia and your best opportunity to enjoy awesome scenery on a day trip from Barcelona. Comprising a massif of limestone pinnacles rising precipitously over gorges, this wondrous place has drawn hermits (er, independent travellers) since the 5th century.

Perched up here is a **monastery** ( ☎ 93 877 70 01; www.abadiamontserrat.net; 🕐 9am-6pm) and a 12th-century chapel built to house **La Moreneta** (the Black Virgin; 🕐 8-10.30am & 12.15-6.30pm Mon-Sat, 8-10.30am, 12.15-6.30pm & 7.30-8.15pm Sun & holidays), a statue found nearby and venerated by hundreds of thousands of people each year. The monastery was founded in 1025. Wrecked by Napoleon's troops in 1811, then abandoned in the 1830s, it was rebuilt from 1858. Today a community of about 80 monks lives here.

The **Museu de Montserrat** ( ☎ 93 877 77 77; Plaça de Santa Maria; adult/student €6.50/5.50; 🕐 10am-6pm) has a varied collection ranging from an Egyptian mummy to works by Degas and Caravaggio. The **Espai Audiovisual** (adult/senior & student €2/1.50, with Museu de Montserrat free; 🕐 9am-6pm) is a walk-through multimedia space that illustrates the monks' daily life.

To see where the holy image of the Virgin was discovered, take the **Funicular de Santa Cova** (one way/return €1.70/2.70; 🕐 every 20min 10am-5.35pm Apr-Oct, 11am-4.25pm

cream-hued lines and flawless service. You might allow yourself to be taken aback by such items as the Big Duck, a hamburger of duck meat.

# DRINK

## BERLIN *Bar*

☎ 93 200 65 42; Carrer de Muntaner 240; ⏰ 10am-1am Mon-Wed, to 3am Thu-Sat; Ⓜ Diagonal or Hospital Clínic

This elegant corner bar with pavement tables also has designer lounges downstairs for sprawling while slurping. There is a relaxed feeling about the place, with a mixed group of customers,

many leaning on the beautiful side and revving up for some clubbing nearby when unceremoniously asked to move on at closing time.

## MARCEL *Bar*

☎ 93 209 89 48; Carrer de Santaló 42; ⏰ 10am-2am Mon-Thu, to 3am Fri & Sat; ⓡ FGC Muntaner

Marcel has a homey but classy old-world feel, with timber bar, black-and-white floor tiles and high windows. It offers a few snacks and tapas, too. Space in this uptown bar is limited and drinkers inevitably spill out onto the pavement.

Nov-Mar) down from the road that runs into the main square and church. The **Funicular de Sant Joan** (one way/return €4.15/6.60; ⏰ every 20min 10am-7pm mid-Jul–Aug, 10am-5.40pm Apr–mid-Jul, Sep & Oct, 11am-4.30pm Nov–Mar) will carry you from the monastery 250m up the mountain in seven minutes. If you prefer to walk, the road leading past the funicular's bottom station winds 3km up the mountain and around to the top station. Children pay about half price on the funiculars.

You can explore the mountain above the monastery by a network of paths leading to some of the peaks and to 13 little chapels. From the Sant Joan top station, it's a 20-minute stroll (signposted) to the Sant Joan chapel. More exciting is the hour's walk northwest along a path marked with occasional blobs of yellow paint to Montserrat's highest peak, Sant Jeroni (1236m), from which there's an awesome sheer drop on the north side.

From Barcelona, the R5 line trains operated by **FGC** (www.fgc.net) run from Plaça d'Espanya station to Monistrol de Montserrat. They connect with the **cremallera** (rack-and-pinion train; www.cremalleradMontserrat.com). One way/return from Barcelona to Montserrat on the FGC train and *cremallera* costs €8.70/15.70. For various all-in ticket options, see the *cremallera* website.

# ⭐ PLAY

## ⭐ BIKINI *Live Music*
www.bikinibcn.com; Carrer de Déu i Mata 105; admission €14; 🕐 midnight-6am Wed-Sun; Ⓜ Maria Cristina

Three main spaces define this, one of the grand old stars of the Barcelona nightlife scene. Every possible kind of music gets a run, depending on the space you choose and the night. From Latin and Brazilian hip-jigglers to 1980s disco, from funk to hip-hop, it all happens here.

## ⭐ BÚCARO *Bar-Club*
☎ 93 209 65 62; Carrer d'Aribau 195; admission Fri & Sat €10; 🕐 11pm-4am Sun-Wed, to 6am Fri & Sat; Ⓜ Diagonal

The doormen are pretty relaxed at this bar-cum-club. The long lounge area where you enter is great for sipping and chilling, while out the back the music makes conversation redundant and close-in dancing inevitable. Upstairs is another quieter bar area.

## ⭐ ELEPHANT *Club*
☎ 93 334 02 58; www.elephantbcn.com in Spanish; Passeig dels Til.lers 1; admission Fri & Sat €15; 🕐 11pm-3am Wed, to 5am Thu-Sun; Ⓜ Palau Reial; Ⓟ

If you can manage to turn up here in a convertible, so much the better. This is like being invited to a celeb's garden party. Inside the big tentlike dance space things can heat up musically as the night wears on, but plenty of people just hang in the gardens with their cocktails.

## ⭐ LUZ DE GAS
*Live Music, Club*
☎ 93 209 77 11; www.luzdegas.com; Carrer de Muntaner 244-246; admission up to €15; 🕐 11.30pm-6am; Ⓜ Diagonal

Anything goes at this large and happening music hall, which hosts residencies and big international names of soul, country, salsa, rock, jazz, pop and cabaret in a beautiful belle époque setting. The versatile place converts into a thumping club with something of a meat-market reputation. Next door, in Sala B, the pace is slower and the bars plentiful over two floors.

## ⭐ MIRABLAU
*Bar-Club*
☎ 93 418 58 79; Plaça del Doctor Andreu, Tibidabo; 🕐 bar 11am-6am; 🚋 FGC Av Tibidabo, then Tramvia Blau or taxi

For the most stunning views of Barcelona – and the spectacle of the city's rich and famous dancing badly – head for this chichi bar and club. Doormen come on for the club at 11pm, and it helps if you're wearing Prada to get past them. One problem with this place is getting away without your own wheels – taxis are not guaranteed.

### ⭐ OTTO ZUTZ *Club*
☎ 93 238 07 22; www.ottozutz.es; Carrer de Lincoln 15; admission €15; ⏱ midnight-5.30am Tue-Sat; ⓇFGC Gràcia

This converted three-storey warehouse remains one of the sexiest and snootiest dance dens in Barcelona. There's a different vibe on each of the three floors (the top floor is for VIPs only), which are linked by a giant atrium.

### ⭐ SUTTON THE CLUB *Club*
☎ 93 414 42 17; www.thesuttonclub .com; Carrer de Tuset 13; admission €15; ⏱ 11.30pm-6am Tue-Sat; Ⓜ Diagonal

An uptown honey pot, this place doesn't get happening until surrounding bars start closing their doors. It's a den of hedonistic beautiful people, and the central dance area (complete with go-go girls and boys), surrounded arena-style by seating and several strategically placed bars, will draw you in.

For those who don't want to meander randomly in Barcelona's several labyrinths, this chapter provides the keys to the city. Whether you want to find Gaudí monuments, zero in on the nightlife, locate districts stacked with eating options or make a last-minute hotel booking, the following pointers can help with everything from feasting to folk dancing.

Escribà patisserie (p51) on La Rambla

# ACCOMMODATION

Hotel construction in Barcelona continues apace but the city still registers high occupation rates. Some 40 more hotels are under construction or planned from 2008 to 2011! It can get tight when trade fairs are on (which is a lot of the time), so booking is warmly recommended. The city is compact, so wherever you choose to stay you will never be too far from the action.

The Barri Gòtic, especially on and around La Rambla and Carrer de Ferran, is jammed with mostly cheapish *hostales* (budget hotels), and generally attracts a boisterous, young, budget crowd. A similar tale applies to El Raval. There are some notable high-end exceptions. The single biggest disadvantage of many of these places can be nocturnal street noise, as revellers fill the night air with their rocket-fuelled cheer.

A growing range of options is sprinkled about the busy La Ribera district and the waterfront. Betting on the business crowd, a huddle of high-rise luxury hotels is gathered in the El Fòrum area, at the city's extreme northeast. When the conference and congress crowd isn't around, prices in these near-new establishments tend to tumble as they scramble for custom. You are about 20 minutes from the city centre by Metro and while the ambience here isn't great, you could easily find yourself with a cheap high-rise room in four-star comfort, with spectacular sea views to boot.

All sorts of hotels are scattered across l'Eixample. This is an extensive area and, depending on what you choose, you will be either just a short stroll outside the old city centre or several Metro stops away. You might decide to take a room in a slightly fusty, old-style *pensión* (small-scale hotel) or *hostal* along Rambla de Catalunya, or opt for a bright, new, modern midrange number or a luxury location with a rooftop pool and gourmet restaurant.

---

**lonely planet** Hotels & Hostels

Need a place to stay? Find and book it at lonelyplanet.com. Over 50 properties are featured for Barcelona – each personally visited, thoroughly reviewed and happily recommended by a Lonely Planet author. From hostels to high-end hotels, we've hunted out the places that will bring you unique and special experiences. Read independent reviews by authors and other travellers, and get practical information including amenities, maps and photos. Then reserve your room simply and securely via Hotels & Hostels – our online booking service. It's all at lonelyplanet.com/hotels.

## WEB RESOURCES

A good website for seeking out some of the city's more striking hotels is **Splendia** (www.splendia.com). Otherwise, book on the city's **tourist-office site** (www.barcelonaturisme.com).

An increasingly popular option is short-term apartment rentals. Agencies and websites offering these abound. They include **Barcelona Online** (www.barcelona-on-line.es), **Apartment Barcelona** (www.apartmentbarcelona.com), **Feelathomebarcelona.com** (www.feelathomebarcelona.com), **Lodging Barcelona** (www.lodgingbarcelona.com), **Rent a Flat in Barcelona** (www.rentaflatinbarcelona.com) and **Oh-Barcelona.Com** (www.oh-barcelona.com). If you're looking to do a short-term house swap, check the ads on **Loquo** (www.loquo.com). Want to sleep on a local's couch? Try **Couch Surfing** (www.couchsurfing.com).

### BEST FOR VIEWS & POOLS
> Hotel Arts Barcelona (www.ritzcarlton.com)
> Hotel Rey Juan Carlos I (www.hrjuancarlos.com)
> Gran Hotel La Florida (www.hotellaflorida.com)
> Grand Marina Hotel (www.grandmarinahotel.com)
> Hotel Claris (www.derbyhotels.es)
> Hotel 54 (www.hotel54barceloneta.com)

### BEST FOR DESIGN
> Hotel Omm (www.hotelomm.es)
> Hotel Banys Orientals (www.hotelbanysorientals.com)
> Hotel Claris (www.derbyhotels.es)
> Casa Camper (www.camper.com)
> Hotel Prestige (www.prestigepaseodegracia.com)
> Market Hotel (www.markethotel.com.es)
> Grand Hotel Central (www.grandhotelcentral.com)

### BEST FOR HISTORY
> Hotel Neri (www.hotelneri.com)
> Hotel 1898 (www.nnhotels.es)
> Hotel Casa Fuster (www.hotelcasafuster.com)
> Hotel Palace (www.hotelpalacebarcelona.com)
> Hotel San Agustin (www.hotelsa.com)
> Chic & Basic (www.chicandbasic.com)

### BEST FOR LOWER BUDGETS
> Hostal d'Uxelles (www.hotelduxelles.com)
> Hostal Girona (www.hostalgirona.com)
> Pensió 2000 (www.pensio2000.com)
> Hostal Goya (www.hostalgoya.com)
> Alberg Mare de Déu de Montserrat (www.tujuca.com)
> Alberg Hostel Itaca (www.itacahostel.com)
> Centric Point Hostel (www.centricpointhostel.com)
> Hostel Mambo Tango (www.hostelmambotango.com)
> Melon District (www.melondistrict.com)

# SHOPPING & FASHION

Twice a year the exclusive urban fashion salon Bread & Butter attracts hundreds of fashion producers and buyers from around the world to Barcelona. Born in Berlin, the salon transferred to Barcelona in 2006 and is going from strength to strength.

The Bread & Butter fair is a global event but Barcelona has no shortage of its own fashion stars. Prét-à-porter giant Mango is a Barcelona success story. Emerging as one of the hippest local names on the world fashion catwalks is the youthful Custo Dalmau (aka Custo Barcelona), with a rapidly growing chain of stores in Spain and abroad. Other local names or Barcelona-based designers include Antonio Miró, Joaquim Verdú, David Valls, Josep Font, Armand Basi, Purificación García, Konrad Muhr, Sita Murt and TCN.

All the big names of Spanish couture, from Adolfo Domínguez to Zara, are also present and there's barely an international brand that doesn't have outlets in Barcelona.

For high fashion, design, jewellery and many department stores, the main shopping axis starts on Plaça de Catalunya, proceeds up Passeig de Gràcia and turns left (west) into Avinguda Diagonal, along which it proceeds as far as Plaça de la Reina Maria Cristina. The densely packed section between Plaça de Francesc Macià (Map p147, D4) and Plaça de la Reina Maria Cristina (Map p147, B4) is good hunting ground.

The heart of l'Eixample – known as the Quadrat d'Or (Golden Sq) – is jammed with all sorts of glittering shops. La Rambla de Catalunya (Map pp106–7, D4) is lined with chic stores, and it's not just about fashion. Carrer del Consell de Cent (Map pp106–7, D4) bursts with art galleries and the nearby streets are also busy with shopping options, from specialist wine purveyors to bookstores.

Shopkeepers in the Barri Gòtic think of their area as 'Barnacentre' (from Barna – slang for Barcelona). Some of the most curious old stores, whether milliners or candle-makers, lurk in the narrow lanes around Plaça de Sant Jaume (Map p43, C3). The once-seedy Carrer d'Avinyó (Map p43, D4) has become a minor fashion boulevard, with creations by up-and-coming designers for a young (and young at heart) clientele. Antique stores abound on and around Carrer de la Palla (Map p43, B2) and Carrer dels Banys Nous (Map p43, B3).

Over in La Ribera there are two categories of shops to look out for: some fine old traditional stores dealing in speciality foodstuffs; and a new crop of fashion and design stores (particularly along the stretch of Carrer del Rec between Passeig del Born and Avinguda del Marquès de l'Argentera; Map pp76–7, E4) catering to the young professionals who have moved into the *barri*. Old-time stores abound in El Raval, where you'll also discover a cluster of preloved clothes shops on Carrer de la Riera Baixa (Map p63, B4).

Non-EU residents are entitled to a refund of the 16% IVA (the Spanish equivalent of VAT or GST) on purchases of more than €90.16 from any shop if they take the goods out of the EU within three months. Ask the shop for a Cashback (or similar) refund form, which you present (with goods, prior to check-in) at the customs booth for IVA refunds when you leave Spain. At Barcelona airport, look for the customs booth opposite the bar on the ground floor of Terminal A.

## MADE FOR WALKING
> Camper (p114)
> Farrutx (p115)

## WHERE FOODIES GO TO HEAVEN
> Caelum (p50)
> Escribà (p51)
> Casa Gispert (p81)
> El Magnífico (p82)
> La Botifarreria (p82)
> Vila Viniteca (p83)
> Mas Bacus (p118)

## FOR FASHIONISTAS
> Custo Barcelona (p82; pictured above)
> Antonio Miró (p114)
> Armand Basi (p114)
> Josep Font (p117)
> Mango (p117)

## WORDS & SOUNDS
> Antinous (p50)
> Altaïr (p113)
> Casa del Llibre (p114)
> Laie (p117)
> Castelló (p66)
> Etnomusic (p66)

# ARCHITECTURE

Leaving aside Antoni Gaudí for a second, Barcelona is one of Europe's great Gothic treasure chests, and it was largely from these jewels that Gaudí and the Modernistas of the late 19th and early 20th centuries took their inspiration, adapting the old rules and techniques to fit their new ways of seeing and building.

Catalan Gothic took its own unique course. Decoration was used more sparingly than elsewhere and, most significantly, Catalan builders championed breadth over height. Stunning examples include the Palau Reial's Saló del Tinell, the Drassanes (the former shipyards that now house the Museu Marítim) and the glorious Església de Santa Maria del Mar.

Modernisme emerged as a trend in Barcelona during the 1880s, the city's belle époque. While the name suggests a rejection of the old, the pioneers of the style actually delved deep into the past for inspiration, absorbed everything they could and then ripped up the rulebook. For many, Modernisme is synonymous with the name Antoni Gaudí

(1852–1926). His works (starting with the unfinished La Sagrada Família church) are the most daring and well known, but he was by no means alone. Lluís Domènech i Montaner (1850–1923) and Josep Puig i Cadafalch (1867–1957) left a wealth of remarkable buildings across the city. They range from Domènech i Montaner's gorgeous Palau de la Música Catalana to Puig i Cadafalch's playful medieval-Dutch-looking Casa Amatller. The many differences between all their designs underline just how eclectic and individual the Modernisme movement was. For details on a Modernisme pack offering a discount on entry to the main Modernista buildings in town, see p105.

Contemporary Barcelona is proving no slouch either, and a slew of local and international architects continues to contribute daring new elements to the city's skyline. The most spectacular is Jean Nouvel's cucumber-shaped, multicoloured tower, the Torre Agbar. The most visible development has been on the northeast stretch of the coast, now home to the Parc del Fòrum (p100) and the surrounding Diagonal Mar residential district.

## BEST OF GAUDÍ
> La Pedrera (p110)
> Casa Batlló (p105)
> La Sagrada Família (p110)
> Palau Güell (p65)
> Park Güell (p130)

## GOOD NEW LOOKERS
> Torre Agbar by Jean Nouvel (p101)
> Mercat de Santa Caterina by Enric Miralles (p78)
> Macba by Richard Meier (p64)
> Edifici Fòrum by Herzog & de Meuron (p100)
> Edifici de Gas Natural by Enric Miralles (p91)
> Teatre Nacional de Catalunya by Ricard Bofill (p127)

## GOTHIC GREATNESS
> Església de Santa Maria del Mar (p75)
> Museu Marítim (p95)
> Saló del Tinell/Museu d'Història de la Ciutat (p47)
> Museu-Monestir de Pedralbes (p149)
> Museu Picasso (p/9)
> La Catedral (p46)

## MORE MODERNISME
> Palau de la Música Catalana by Lluís Domènech i Montaner (p80)
> Casa Amatller by Josep Puig i Cadafalch (p111)
> Hospital de la Santa Creu i de Sant Pau by Lluís Domènech i Montaner (p109)
> Palau del Baró Quadras – Casa Asia by Josep Puig i Cadafalch (p112)

**Left** Torre Agbar (p101): the big cucumber

SNAPSHOTS

# CATALAN CUISINE

Sure, Barcelona has become a cauldron of culinary kookiness, with the foams and froths of master chef Ferran Adrià and his disciples. But you can still get a taste of yesteryear and traditional Catalan cooking.

Rice is grown in the Delta de l'Ebre area in southern Catalonia and used widely. *Arròs a la cassola* or *arròs a la catalana* is Catalan paella, cooked in an earthenware pot and without saffron, whereas *arròs negre* is rice cooked in cuttlefish ink – much tastier than it sounds. *Fideuà* is similar to paella, but uses noodles rather than rice. You should also receive a little side dish of *allioli* (a mayonnaise-style sauce of pounded garlic with olive oil) to mix in.

Seafood is high on Catalan menus but hearty meat dishes from the interior also figure prominently. *Botifarra* (sausages) come in many shapes and sizes, and for some there's nothing better than a sizzling *solomillo* (sirloin) of *vedella* (beef) prepared *a punto* (medium rare).

Catalans are passionate about *calçots* (large, sweet spring onions), which are barbecued over hot coals, dipped in tangy *romesco* sauce (a finely ground mixture of tomatoes, peppers, onions, garlic, almonds and olive oil) and eaten voraciously when in season from January until March. This is most traditionally done as a Sunday lunch outing in which the *calçots* are the first course, followed by copious meat and sausage dishes as the main.

Typical desserts include *crema catalana,* a delicious version of crème brûlée, but you might also be offered *mel i mató,* honey and fresh cream cheese.

## GOOD OLD-FASHIONED COOKING

> Casa Leopoldo (p68)
> Suquet de l'Almirall (p96)
> Bilbao (p131)
> Cafè de l'Acadèmia (p56)
> Cal Boter (p131)
> La Tomaquera (p143)

# CAFES & RESTAURANTS

In Barcelona, new restaurants and cafes open (and close) with astounding rapidity, although brand spanking new is not always synonymous with good. Never fear, for the choice of good places is overwhelming!

A few old-guard restaurants specialise in traditional Catalan cooking, while other equally venerable establishments, often run by Basques or Galicians, offer a mix of regional specialities and what can loosely be termed 'Spanish cooking'. Such places are scattered across the Barri Gòtic, El Raval and l'Eixample areas. Seafood is also prominent, especially in La Barceloneta. Booking is advisable at midrange and expensive places, especially from Thursday to Saturday.

Cafes and bars abound. Locals tend to take their coffee on the hop at the bar but there's no shortage of places to sit over a hot cuppa and the paper. For sweet teeth, head for a *granja,* where thick hot chocolate is the go!

### BEST FOR PAELLA
> Elche (p143)
> Set (7) Portes (p87)
> Xiringuito d'Escribà (p102)
> Palau de Mar (p96)

### BEST FOR DEALS & DINNERS
> Casa Darío (p121)
> Agut (p56)
> Casa Calvet (p121)
> El Racó d'En Freixa (p152)

### BEST FOR COFFEE & PAPER
> Cafè del Centre (p119)
> Cafè Zurich (p57)
> Cafè de l'Òpera (p56; pictured above)
> Granja Viader (p68)

### BEST FOR VEGETARIANS
> Biocenter (p68)
> Amaltea (p119)
> Sesamo (p69)

# TAPAS

Today's emblematic Spanish bar snacks supposedly originated in Andalucía's sherry area in the 19th century, when bar owners placed a piece of bread on top of a drink to deter flies; this developed into the custom of putting a titbit, such as olives or a piece of sausage (something salty to encourage drinking), on a lid to cover the drink. Since then, tapas have become a cuisine of their own.

Not originally an integral part of the Catalan eating tradition, tapas culture was long ago imported to Barcelona. Particularly popular are the Basque Country versions, *pintxos,* most of which come in the form of canapés. On slices of baguette are perched anything from *bacalao* (cod) to *morcilla* (black pudding). These are most refreshingly washed down with a slightly tart Basque white wine, *txacoli,* which is served like cider to give it a few (temporary) bubbles. Each *pintxo* comes with a toothpick and payment is by the honour system – you keep your toothpicks and present them for the final count when you ask for the bill.

In some gourmet spots, tapas have become something of an art form, while in many straightforward, beery bars you might just get a saucer of olives to accompany your tipple.

## TAPAS TIME

> Cal Pep (p85)
> El Vaso de Oro (p96)
> Inopia (p122)
> Quimet i Quimet (p143)
> Taktika Berri (p123)
> Tapaç 24 (p123)

# NIGHTLIFE

Barcelona knows how to party, but to experience the city in its natural light you'll need to go out late. Barcelonins are still in front of the mirror by the time you're usually in full flight, bars are barely getting into their stride at 10pm and clubs (best on Thursday to Saturday nights) don't come alive before 2am.

The lower end of the Barri Gòtic, the hip El Born area and parts of El Raval (where you'll find many of the city's truly atmospheric old taverns) are all busy, with bars of all descriptions. In l'Eixample, the main axis is along Carrer d'Aribau (Map pp106–7, B4) and into the chichi Zona Alta area around Carrer de Tuset and Carrer de Marià Cubí (Map p147, D4) – an area that attracts the bulk of Barcelona's *pijos* (the smart, well-financed crowd). The squares and some streets of Gràcia also hop, largely with a young, local crowd.

A handful of clubs are dotted on or near Plaça Reial in the Barri Gòtic (Map p43, B4) and there are a couple each in El Raval and Poble Sec. Revellers in El Born often make for the Port Olímpic end of La Barceloneta for dancing. Most locals, however, will contest that the classier places are in La Zona Alta.

For nightlife info, check out **Guía del Ocio** (www.guiadelociobcn.es), available from newsstands (€1). *Micro, Go Mag, Mondo Sonoro, Nit, Gig* and *Salir* (all in Spanish) are free at bars. See Forward Planning, p36, for a list of websites.

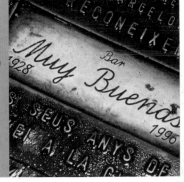

## TIPPLING WITH HISTORY
> Bar Marsella (p69)
> London Bar (p72)
> Casa Almirall (p72)
> Bar Muy Buenas (p70; pictured right)
> Bar Pastís (p70)

## BEST CLUBS
> Luz de Gas (p154)
> Opium Mar (p103)
> Otto Zutz (p155)
> Sutton The Club (p155)
> Terrrazza (p145)

SNAPSHOTS

# PUBLIC ART

The streets, squares and parks of Barcelona are littered with the signatures of artists past and present, famous and unknown. They range from Modernista sculptors, like Josep Llimona, to international star sculptors, such as Roy Lichtenstein and Fernando Botero. Picasso and Joan Miró both left lasting reminders in the city.

Since the return of democracy in the late 1970s, the town hall has not been shy about encouraging the placement of sometimes grandiose and often equally incomprehensible contemporary works in the city's public spaces. Reactions range from admiration to perplexity.

Justly proud of its rich street-art heritage, the council has also created an extensive archive of it all on the internet at www.bcn.cat (click on Art Públic, under Blog Barcelona). The site is rich in description of hundreds of items scattered across the city, and includes commentary on the history of the city through its street art. You can search particular items by district, period and key word.

The best thing about art in the streets is that it is open to all comers. Of the many hundreds of statues and other works around town, we list some outstanding pieces here.

**FREE FOR ALL**
> Barcelona Head (p94)
> David i Goliat (p100)
> Dona i Ocell (p141)
> El Desconsol (p81)
> Gat (p64; pictured right)
> Homenatge a la Barceloneta (p91)

# CONTEMPORARY ART

Three of the great names in 20th-century art are associated with Barcelona, and two left behind considerable legacies in the city. Having admired early Picasso and the breadth of Miró's work in their respective Barcelona museums, it would be a shame to miss the loopiness of that doyen of daftness, Salvador Dalí, a train ride away in Figueres (p140).

In the wake of the big three, Barcelona has been a minor cauldron of activity, dominated by the figure of Antoni Tàpies (b 1923). Early in his career (from the mid-1940s onwards) he seemed keen on self-portraits, but also experimented with collage using all sorts of materials, from wood to rice.

A poet, artist and man of theatre, Joan Brossa (1921–98) was a cultural beacon in Barcelona. His 'visual poems', lithographs and other artworks in which letters generally figure, along with all sorts of objects, make his world accessible to those who can't read his Catalan poetry.

Joan Hernández Pijuan (1931–2005), one of Barcelona's most important 20th-century abstract painters, produced work concentrating on natural shapes and figures, often using neutral colours on different surfaces.

Jaume Plensa (b 1955) is possibly Spain's best contemporary sculptor. His work ranges from sketches, through sculpture, to video and other installations that have been shown around the world. Susana Solano (b 1946), one of Barcelona's best painters and sculptors, also works with video installations, collages and jewellery. Jordi Colomer (b 1962) makes heavy use of audiovisual material in his artworks, creating highly imaginative spaces and three-dimensional images.

## ART FOR ART'S SAKE

> For a selection of Tàpies' works and contemporary art exhibitions – Fundació Antoni Tàpies (p109)
> For a private, diverse art collection – Fundación Francisco Godia (p109)
> For Joan Brossa's eclectic work – Fundació Joan Brossa (p109)
> For Joan Miró – Fundació Joan Miró (p135)
> For early Picasso – Museu Picasso (p79)

> For contemporary art – Museu d'Art Contemporani de Barcelona (Macba; p64)
> For a modest collection of ancient Egyptian art – Museu Egipci (p112)
> For Romanesque sculpture – Museu Frederic Marès (p48)
> For the gamut of Catalan art – Museu Nacional d'Art de Catalunya (MNAC; p140)

# FLAMENCO

The stirring sounds of flamenco, a cultural hybrid mixing the music of *gitanos* (Roma) with other influences (from North African Berber music to Gregorian chants and traditional medieval Jewish music), are usually associated with Andalucía in southern Spain. But the *gitanos* who arrived in Spain from India in the Middle Ages were also present in Catalonia. Records of *gitanos* performing in Barcelona date from the 19th century, when the music came to prominence across the country. Perhaps the best-known flamenco dancer born in Catalonia and associated with Barcelona was Carmen Amaya (1913–63).

A peculiarly Barcelona phenomenon is Rumba Catalana. In the 1950s a new sound mixing flamenco with Latin (salsa and other South American dance flavours) emerged in *gitano* circles in Gràcia and the Barri Gòtic. The main man was Antonio González, known as El Pescaílla (and married to the flamenco star Lola Flores). Mataró-born *gitano* Peret took it to wider, international audiences. By the end of the 1970s, however, Rumba Catalana was out of steam. Today, new rumba bands have emerged: watch out for Papawa, Barrio Negro and El Tío Carlos. An exciting Barcelona combo is Ojos de Brujo (Wizard's Eyes), who meld flamenco and rumba with rap, ragga and electronic music.

For more on flamenco in Barcelona see www.flamencobarcelona .com (in Spanish). Listed below are some names in contemporary Catalan flamenco worth looking out for.

## CATALAN FIRE
> Juan Cortés Duquende
> Miquel Poveda
> Ginesa Ortega Cortés
> Montse Cortés
> Mayte Martín

# SARDANA

Catalans take their national dance, the *sardana,* seriously (it is not a dance accompanied by peals of laughter). Dancers gather to form a circle, usually piling up their bags and other chattels in the middle. All hold hands and execute a series of complex steps, bobbing up and down and heading right and left. At first glance, it has something in common with other Mediterranean dances in the round, but it is generally a sober affair.

The accompanying music, by turns melancholic and jolly, is played by a reed-and-brass band called a *cobla,* and most of it was written by the 19th century. The origins of the dance are unclear, but the first written reference appeared in the 16th century. Popular assurances that the *sardana* was banned under Franco are hotly disputed by those who have taken the trouble to study the period.

Many Catalans will quietly confess they are not great fans of this folk dancing, but as an affirmation of Catalan identity it has its own particular charm. And many seem to genuinely enjoy it. The steps are more complicated that is at first apparent, but locals will be more than chuffed if you wish to learn!

The most likely chance you'll have of seeing a *sardana* is in front of La Catedral (p46), at 7pm on Wednesday, from 6.30pm to 8.30pm on Saturday, and from noon to 2pm on Sunday. You can also see the dance during some of the city's festivals.

So you think you can dance? *Sardana* dancing in the Barri Gòtic

SNAPSHOTS

# GAY & LESBIAN BARCELONA

Barcelona has a busy gay scene, as does Sitges on the coast to the south-west. In Barcelona, the bulk of the action happens in an area about five to six blocks southwest of Passeig de Gràcia, around Carrer del Consell de Cent (Map pp106–7, C5). Sitges (p140), meanwhile, attracts an international gay crowd from Easter to the tail end of summer, and comes to life with a bang for Carnaval (Carnival) in February, when it puts on outrageous parades around town.

Same-sex marriages were legalised in 2005, and a Catalan gay couple became the first in Spain to legally adopt a child in mid-2006.

**Casal Lambda** (Map pp76-7, B3; ☎ 93 319 55 50; www.lambdaweb.org; Carrer de Verdaguer i Callis 10; Ⓜ Urquinaona) is a gay and lesbian social centre. The **Coordinadora Gai-Lesbiana** (Map p147, C5; ☎ 93 298 00 29; www.cogailes.org; Carrer de Violant d'Hongria 156; Ⓜ Plaça del Centre) is the city's main coordinating body for gay and lesbian groups. **GayBarcelona.com** (www.gaybarcelona.com) has news and views and an extensive listings section.

## BEST GAY STAYS
> Hotel Axel (www.axelhotels.com)
> Hotel California (www.hotelcalifornia bcn.com)

## BARS & CLUBS
> Arena Madre (p125)
> DBoy (p126)
> Dietrich Gay Teatro Café (p124)
> La Chapelle (p125)
> Metro (p126)

# BEACHES

Barcelona's reputation as a metropolitan seaside resort is justified and yet artificial. (That is, the beaches are artificial.)

Starting from the southwest end of town, Platja de Sant Miquel (Map pp92–3) is, from the mid-afternoon, a gay-male nudist strip, although very relaxed. Platja de Sant Sebastià and Platja de la Barceloneta are more family affairs. The five beaches stretching northeast from Port Olímpic (starting with Platja de Nova Icària; Map p99) have nicer sand and cleaner water. All have at least one *chiringuito* – snacks and drinks bars that are often open until 1am (Easter to October).

Frankly, though, the beaches outside Barcelona are far superior. Northeast of the city, the train to Blanes zips past beach after beach along the Costa del Maresme. Some have an urban flavour; others are more tucked away. The sand is sandier and the water noticeably more transparent the further you get from the city.

To the southwest, the beaches of the Costa del Garraf and Costa Daurada tend to be broad, flat affairs. The further south you head, the less chance you have of encountering even a speck of cloud. Apart from Platja d'Altafulla and Cala de la Mora, all can be reached by train.

## COSTA DEL MARESME FAVOURITES
> Caldes d'Estrac
> Arenys de Mar
> Canet de Mar
> Sant Pol de Mar
> Platja dels Pins (Malgrat de Mar)

## SOUTHWEST FAVOURITES
> Garraf
> Sitges
> Cubelles
> Platja d'Altafulla
> Cala de la Mora (Tamarit)

# FOOTBALL

Football has something of the status of religion in Barcelona. Indeed, in this traditionally rose-tinged town (with a serious conservative overlay in its entrepreneurial class), one is tempted to see the Camp Nou football stadium (see Follow the Balls, p148) as the principal temple of worship. The object of such ecstasy is **Football Club Barcelona** (www.fcbarcelona.com), one of the most exciting teams in Europe and a bastion of Catalan identity (in spite of the majority of players being from abroad).

It all started on 29 November 1899, when Swiss Hans Gamper founded FC Barcelona (Barça), four years after English residents had first played the game here. His choice of club colours – the blue and maroon of his home town, Winterthur – has stuck. By 1910 FC Barcelona was the premier club in a rapidly growing league. The first signs of professionalism emerged: paid transfers of players were recorded and the management of the city's other emerging club, Espanyol, charged spectators. Barça had 560 members (it has about 156,000 today), who were all chuffed at the team's victory at that year's national championship.

Barça is one of only three teams (Real Madrid and Athletic de Bilbao are the others) never to have been relegated to the 2nd division. That said, it had a horrible year in 2007–08, failing to win a single competition or cup, despite coming close on several occasions.

**Espanyol** (www.rcdespanyol.com), based for now at the Estadi Olímpic while its new stadium is built, traditionally plays a quiet second fiddle to Barça.

Camp Nou stadium (p148), home to FC Barcelona

# KIDS IN BARCELONA

In summer especially, kids will love Barcelona's beaches, pools and parks. Quite a few of the sights are bound to fascinate them, too, and the sheer theatre of central Barcelona's streets will keep them agog.

One of the great things about Barcelona is the inclusion of children in many apparently adult activities. Going out to eat or sipping a beer on a late summer evening at a *terraza* (terrace) needn't mean leaving children with minders. Locals take their kids out all the time and don't worry about keeping them up late.

Most of the mid- and upper-range hotels in Barcelona can organise a babysitting service. A company that many hotels use and that you can also contact directly is **5 Serveis** ( ☎ 93 412 56 76; Carrer de Pelai 50). It has multilingual babysitters *(canguros)*. Rates vary, but in the evening expect to pay around €10 an hour plus the cost of a taxi home for the babysitter. **Tender Loving Canguros** ( ☎ 647 605989; www.tlcanguros.com) offers English-speaking babysitters for a minimum of three hours (€7 an hour).

You could take younger kiddies (maximum age 11) to **Happy Parc** (Map pp106-7, E4; ☎ 93 317 86 60; www.happyparc.com in Catalan; Carrer de Pau Claris 97; per hr €4; ⏰ 5-9pm Mon-Fri, 11am-9pm Sat & Sun) for a play on the slides and other diversions.

The listed sights should please most kids of most ages.

## TOPS FOR KIDS

> l'Aquàrium (p91)
> beaches (p173)
> Parc del Fòrum & Zona de Banys (p100)
> Parc d'Atraccions (p150)
> Zoo de Barcelona (p81)
> Poble Espanyol (p142)
> Transbordador Aeri (p95)
> Golondrina excursion boats (p91)
> Parc de la Ciutadella (p80)

## MUSEUMS FOR MINORS

> CosmoCaixa (p148)
> Museu de Cera (p46)
> Museu Marítim (p95)
> Museu de la Xocolata (p79)
> Castell de Montjuïc & Museu Militar (p135)

# BULLFIGHTING

In 2004 the city council narrowly voted for a symbolic declaration that Barcelona was anti-bullfighting. Animal-rights groups and many Catalans, who consider *la lidia* (bullfighting) a cultural imposition from Spain, were delighted. The vote was divisive because, like it or not, bullfighting has a long history in Barcelona.

Bullfighting is by no means an exclusively Castilian (central Spanish) activity. It has a long history in Portugal and southern France, and is especially popular in the Basque Country. Indeed, spectacles involving bullbaiting in one form or another were common in other parts of Europe and rooted in the legacy of such 'games' under the Roman Empire.

The first bullfight in Barcelona was held in 1387, long before Catalonia was subordinated to Castilian overlordship. And Catalans may or may not be less enthusiastic about bullfighting than other Spaniards (vegetarian anarchists banned it during the civil war in Barcelona), but this doesn't stop them from staging a season at the **Plaça de Braus Monumental bullring** (Map pp106-7, G2; ☎ 93 245 58 02; cnr Gran Via de les Corts Catalanes & Carrer de la Marina; Ⓜ Monumental), usually on Sundays in spring and summer. Local *toreros* (bullfighters) include Manolo Porcel and Serafín Marin. Occasional performances at the bullring by the big-name bullfighters are major events. Tickets are available at the **arena** (🕙 11am-2pm & 4-8pm Mon-Sat, 10am-6pm Sun), through **ServiCaixa** ( ☎ 902 332211; www.servicaixa.com) or at **Toros Taquilla Oficial** (Map pp106-7, C5; Carrer de Muntaner 26; 🕙 11am-2pm & 4-8pm Wed-Fri, 11am-2pm & 4-7pm Sat; Ⓜ Universitat).

There are rumours that the bullring might be converted into the new site of Els Encants Vells market (p115).

## STARS OF THE RING
> José Tomás
> Julián López ('El Juli')
> José Miguel Arroyo ('Joselito')
> Manuel Jesús ('El Cid')
> David Fandila ('El Fandi')
> Manuel Díaz ('El Cordobés')

Antoni Tàpies' wire sculpture *Núvol i Cadira* (Cloud and Chair) crowning Fundació Antoni Tàpies (p109)

# BACKGROUND

## HISTORY

### WILFRED THE HAIRY & MEDITERRANEAN EXPANSION

The Romans put Barcino on the map in the 3rd century BC. They were followed by the Visigoths, Moors and Franks, who in the 9th century AD put the city under the control of local counts as a buffer zone against Muslim-dominated Spain.

Count Guifré el Pelós (Wilfred the Hairy) wrested control over several neighbouring territories in what later became known as Catalonia, and by 878 Barcelona was its key city. He founded a dynasty that lasted nearly five centuries. After the Franks failed to help Barcelona repel a Muslim assault in 985, the region became independent of Frankish suzerainty.

The counts of Barcelona gradually expanded their territory south, expelling the Muslims from what is now southern Catalonia. In 1137 Ramon Berenguer IV, the Count of Barcelona, married Petronilla, heiress to the throne of neighbouring Aragón, and thus created the combined Crown of Aragón. In the following centuries the regime became a flourishing merchant empire, seizing Valencia and the Balearic Islands from the Muslims, and later taking territories as far flung as Sardinia, Sicily and parts of Greece.

### CASTILIAN DOMINANCE

Overstretched, racked by civil disobedience and decimated by the Black Death, Catalonia began to wobble by the 14th century. When the last count of Wilfred the Hairy's dynasty expired without leaving an heir, the Crown of Aragón was passed to a noble of Castile. Soon these two Spanish kingdoms merged, with Catalonia left as a very junior partner. As business shifted from the Mediterranean to the Atlantic after the discovery of the Americas in 1492, Catalans were increasingly marginalised from trade.

### ROUGH JUSTICE

Medieval Catalonia developed its own system of laws, the Usatges, based on Roman-Visigothic precepts and feudal custom in the 11th century. It could be a little rough: '...let them (the rulers) render justice as it seems fit to them: by cutting off hands and feet, putting out eyes, keeping men in prison for a long time and, ultimately, in hanging their bodies if necessary... In regard to women, let the rulers render justice by cutting off their noses, lips, ears and breasts, and by burning them at the stake if necessary...' One wonders what the definition of necessary was.

The region, which had retained some autonomy in the running of its own affairs, was dealt a crushing blow when it supported the wrong side in the War of the Spanish Succession (1702–14) and the Bourbon king, Felipe V, established a unitary Castilian state. He banned the writing and teaching of Catalan, swept away the remnants of local legal systems and tore down a whole district of medieval Barcelona in order to construct an immense fort (on the site of the present-day Parc de la Ciutadella; p80), whose sole purpose was to watch over Barcelona's troublemakers.

## ECONOMIC GROWTH & THE RENAIXENÇA

Buoyed by the lifting of the ban on its trade with the Americas in 1778, Barcelona embarked on the road to industrial revolution, based initially on textiles but spreading to wine, cork and iron in the mid-19th century. It soon became Spain's leading city. As the economy prospered, Barcelona outgrew its medieval walls, which were demolished in 1854–56. Work on the grid-plan Eixample (Extension) district began soon after. The so-called Renaixença (Renaissance) brought a revival of Catalan culture, as well as political activism, and sowed the seeds of growing political tension in the early 20th century, as demands for autonomy from the central state became more insistent.

## ANARCHY, CIVIL WAR & FRANCO

Adding to the fiery mix was growing discontent among the working class. The grand Catalan merchant-bourgeois families grew richer, displaying their wealth in a slew of whimsical private mansions built with verve and flair by Modernista (Catalan Art Nouveau) architects such as Antoni Gaudí. At the same time, the industrial working class, housed in cramped quarters such as La Barceloneta and El Raval, and oppressed by poverty and disease, became organised and on occasion violent. Spain's neutrality during WWI had boosted Barcelona's economy, and from 1900 to 1930 the population doubled to one million, but the postwar global slump hit the city hard. Waves of strikes, organised principally by the anarchists' Confederación Nacional del Trabajo, brought tough responses. Left-wing and right-wing gangs took their ideological conflict to the streets. Tit-for-tat assassinations became common currency and the death toll mounted.

When the Second Spanish Republic was created under a left-wing government in 1931, Catalonia declared independence. Later, under pressure, its leaders settled for devolution, which it then lost in 1934, when a right-wing government won power in Madrid. The election of a left-wing popular front in 1936 again sparked Catalan autonomy claims but also led General Franco to launch the Spanish Civil War (1936–39), from which he emerged the victor. Barcelona, which for much of the war was the acting capital of Spain, was regularly bombed from March 1938 onwards, mostly by Fascist Italian aircraft based in Franco-occupied Mallorca.

Barcelona was run by anarchists and the Partido Obrero de Unificación Marxista (Marxist Unification Workers' Party) Trotskyist militia until mid-1937. Unions took over factories and public services, hotels and mansions became hospitals and schools, everyone wore workers' clothes, bars and cafes were collectivised, trams and taxis were painted red and black (the colours of the anarchists), and one-way streets were ignored as they were seen to be part of the old system.

The more radical anarchists were behind the burning of most of the city's churches and the shooting of more than 1200 priests, monks and nuns. The anarchists in turn were shunted aside by the communists (directed by Stalin from Moscow) after a bloody internecine battle in Barcelona that left 1500 dead in May 1937. Later that year, the Spanish republican government fled Valencia and made Barcelona the official capital (the government had left besieged Madrid early in the war).

The Republican defeat at the hands of the Nationalists in the Battle of the Ebro in southern Catalonia in summer 1938 left Barcelona undefended. It fell to the Nationalists on 25 January 1939, triggering a mass exodus of refugees to France, where most were long interned in makeshift camps.

Purges and executions under Franco continued until well into the 1950s. Former Catalan president Lluís Companys was arrested in France by the Gestapo in August 1940, handed over to Franco, and shot on 15 October on Montjuïc. He is reputed to have died with the words *'Visca Catalunya!'* ('Long live Catalonia!') on his lips.

## THE CITY REBORN

The Francoist Josep Maria de Porcioles was mayor from 1957 until his death in 1973, a grey time for Barcelona marked by regular demonstrations against the regime, always brutally put down. When Franco himself died two years later, the city rejoiced. In 1977 Catalonia was granted regional autonomy.

In 1980, in the first free regional elections since before the civil war, wily Catalan nationalist Jordi Pujol was elected president of Catalonia at the head of the Convergència i Unió coalition. He remained at the controls until 2003, when he stepped down and was succeeded by the former socialist mayor of Barcelona, Pasqual Maragall. Maragall's rocky three-party coalition stumbled in 2006, and he was replaced by socialist colleague José Montilla, who remains at the head of an uneasy coalition government today.

The 1992 Olympics marked the beginning of a long process of urban renewal. The waterfront, beaches and Montjuïc were in the first wave, but the momentum hasn't been lost since. The Ciutat Vella (Old City) continues to be spruced up, and a determined campaign to repair the city's facades is lending Barcelona a brighter feel. Ambitious projects like the 22@bcn hi-tech zone in the once-industrial El Poblenou district, the major development around new trade-fair grounds between the city and the airport, and the fancy Diagonal Mar waterfront development around the Parc del Fòrum at the northeast tip of the city are just a few examples of Barcelona's urban dynamism.

# LIFE IN BARCELONA

Spain's second city, Barcelona counts 1.6 million inhabitants, with another 3.6 million crammed into the province around the city. The loosely defined 'greater Barcelona area' is home to about 4.7 million people.

While much of the rest of Catalonia is largely Catalan in identity, Barcelona is a mixed bag. Massive internal migration in the 1950s and '60s brought 1.5 million Spaniards from other parts of the country to the capital and surrounding areas. Many of those families still prefer to speak Spanish over Catalan today.

The more affluent parts of the city and some central districts retain a predominantly Catalan flavour, but things are changing. Rapidly increasing immigration from abroad is altering the city's face. Almost 15% of the officially resident population are foreigners (35% in the Ciutat Vella).

The overwhelming majority of new arrivals are South Americans, but there are also sizable contingents from Morocco and Pakistan (mostly living in El Raval), as well as Eastern Europe (especially Romania and Bulgaria) and China. Many are *clandestinos* (illegal). Throw in a good number of arrivals from affluent northern European countries in search of the good life, and the mix is heady.

Nominally, most Catalans are Catholics, although one study says that more than half of young Catalans declare themselves nonreligious.

## READING BARCELONA

> *Barcelona*, Robert Hughes – A witty and passionate study by the stormy Australian art critic of the art, architecture and life of the city through history.
> *Homage to Catalonia*, George Orwell – Orwell's classic account of the first half of the 1936–39 Spanish Civil War as he experienced it in Barcelona and on the front line in Catalonia.
> *La Catedral del Mar* (Cathedral of the Sea), Ildefonso Falcones – A historical novel set in medieval Barcelona, telling the story of the construction of the Església de Santa Maria del Mar, a Gothic beauty raised in record (and, for many of its workers, back-breaking) time.
> *La Ciudad de los Prodigios* (The City of Marvels), Eduardo Mendoza – A surreal novel set in Barcelona from the Universal Exhibition of 1888 to the World Exhibition of 1929. Through the story of the ruthless rise to power of its main protagonist, Mendoza paints a broad picture of Barcelona society in this turbulent period.
> *La Sombra del Viento* (The Shadow of the Wind), Carlos Ruiz Zafón – This engaging mystery bestseller plays out over several periods in Barcelona's 20th-century history and is fascinating for anyone who has spent time in the city, or intends to. Zafón followed up in 2008 with *El Juego del Ángel* (The Angel's Game), not quite a sequel but in a similar stylistic vein.
> *Plaça del Diamant* (The Time of the Doves), Mercè Rodoreda – This slow-moving classic follows the life of the city before, during and after the civil war, as seen through the eyes of a local woman born in the Gràcia area.

Barcelona's working class has, since the 19th century, always given the city a politically reddish, anticlerical hue.

# GOVERNMENT & POLITICS

Ever since Spain made its transition from dictatorship to democracy in the wake of Franco's death in 1975, the Barcelona Ajuntament (Town Hall) has been in the hands of the Partit Socialista de Catalunya (PSC), a branch of the nationwide socialist party, the PSOE. In 2007 Jordi Hereu just scraped in as mayor in a minority coalition with Iniciativa Verds–Esquerra Unida (Green Initiative–United Left).

Facing him in opposition are the right-wing, Catalan-nationalist Convergència i Unió (CiU) coalition and the avowedly left-wing, independence-minded Esquerra Republicana de Catalunya (ERC, Republican Left of Catalonia). The CiU and ERC are doing their level best to block Hereu at every turn. Both did an about-face and voted to freeze plans for a controversial high-speed rail tunnel across central Barcelona, but given that the tunnel has already been given the go-ahead, these votes amount to little more than grandstanding.

The tunnel (which will run below the street next to two Gaudí monuments, La Sagrada Família and La Pedrera, on its 6km route between Estació Sants and a new transport junction at La Sagrera) has sparked opposition from directly affected residents and management of La Sagrada Família. The latter claims vibrations due to tunnelling and train traffic will imperil Barcelona's number-one cultural sight. The city, regional and national governments reject such claims. Experts are divided, but courts have so far overruled the protests and work began in mid-2008.

Assurances that everything will be all right, however, ring hollow to many Barcelonins after the years of chaos and suffering caused by construction of the high-speed line from Madrid to Estació Sants. Not only did it arrive six years late (in early 2008), but damage to nearby housing, intolerable living conditions as works proceeded 24 hours a day, and the collapse in the latter half of 2007 of the underfunded local train network, suggest to many that those responsible can hardly guarantee problem-free construction of the planned tunnel. And no one has forgotten the 2005 implosion of a metro tunnel under construction in the suburb of El Carmel, which destroyed four apartment blocks and left more than 1200 people homeless.

For years, Barcelona and the regional Catalan government have railed against Madrid's lack of investment in infrastructure in Catalonia, from transport to electricity supply. In addition to the rail chaos, part of the city was plunged into darkness for several days in July 2007 in a chain reaction of burn-outs at city substations.

These mishaps confirm what many a Catalan feels about Spain's national government, regardless of which political colours it flies. A constant complaint from Barcelona is that, under Spain's system of redistribution of resources from better-off to poorer regions, Catalonia has been allowed to decline while financing other regions. In 2006 a new statute granting Catalonia greater autonomy and increased funding was approved by the national parliament and by referendum in Catalonia. By the time of writing, however, it had still largely been left unimplemented, to the growing consternation of Catalonia's PSC president, José Montilla. José Luis Rodríguez Zapatero, the country's socialist president whose March 2008 electoral victory was largely made possible with Catalan votes, has vowed to step up funding for infrastructure in Catalonia, but it appears that some bargaining remains to be done, especially as Spain heads into troubled economic waters. In 2008 the international credit crisis coincided with a collapse in the construction industry in Spain, and national unemployment rose from 8.3% to 11.3% in a year.

# ART

Northern Catalonia is sprinkled with hundreds of early medieval stone churches and chapels. They were once spectacularly filled with bright Romanesque frescoes that served as didactic material for the mostly illiterate faithful. Today, a grand collection of the best of these frescoes can be seen in Barcelona in the Museu Nacional d'Art de Catalunya (MNAC; p140).

Painters of the Romanesque and early Gothic periods were largely anonymous, but later some bright lights began to emerge and sign their works, which were almost always of a religious nature. One of the region's first recognised masters was Ferrer Bassá (c 1290–1348). Influenced by the Italian school of Siena, his few surviving works include murals with a slight touch of caricature in the Museu-Monestir de Pedralbes (p149).

Bernat Martorell (1400–52), a master of chiaroscuro who was active in the mid-15th century, was one of the region's leading exponents of International Gothic, while Jaume Huguet (1415–92) adopted the sombre realism of the Flemish school, lightening the style with Hispanic splashes of gold.

Not until the late 19th century did artists of note again emerge in Catalonia. Led by dandy Ramón Casas (1866–1932) and his pal Santiago Rusiñol (1861–1931), the Modernistas were for a while the talk of the town. At the same time, Málaga-born Pablo Picasso (1881–1973) spent his formative adolescent years in Barcelona, where he did the paintings of his Blue Period. He moved to Paris in 1904, and went on to experiment

## CARVALHO ON THE CASE

Manuel Vázquez Montalbán (1939–2003) was one of Barcelona's most prolific and best-loved writers, whose work ranged from essays on his home city to books on Cuba's Fidel Castro. He is best known for his detective series, featuring Pepe Carvalho. This overweight, somewhat melancholy, food-loving private eye trawls the darker side of Barcelona's streets, but always finds time for a good meal and copious tipples. Oh, and always gets his man. Several of these stories have been published in English, including *South Seas*, *Off Side* and *Murder in the Central Committee* (set outside Barcelona).

## BARCELONA ON FILM

Surprisingly few good films have been set in Barcelona, although a few more have been at least partially shot there. Among the best are the following:

> *Todo Sobre Mi Madre* (All About My Mother), Pedro Almodóvar (1999) – One of the Spanish director's most polished films, mostly set in Barcelona. A quirky commentary that ties together the lives of the most improbable collection of women (including a couple of transsexuals).

> *Vicky Cristina Barcelona,* Woody Allen (2008) – Barcelona was all agog in 2007 as Woody Allen, Scarlett Johansson, Penelope Cruz and Javier Bardem wandered around shooting Allen's vision of Barcelona. Bardem, a painter, gets Cruz and Johansson all hot and sweaty in this light romantic romp.

> *Perfume: The Story of a Murderer,* Tom Tykwer (2006) – Starring Ben Wishaw as the psychopathic Jean-Baptiste Grenouille, this film is based on the extraordinary novel by Patrick Süsskind and partly shot on locations across town and around Catalonia.

> *L'Auberge Espagnole* (The Spanish Apartment), Cédric Klapisch (2002) – A young Parisian from the suburbs, Xavier, goes to Barcelona to learn Spanish for business. It ain't easy when university classes are given half the time in Catalan, but Xavier has no yen to return to Paris.

> *El Gran Gato,* Ventura Pons (2003) – A kind of musical dedicated to the singer-songwriter Javier Patricio 'Gato' Pérez.

> *Gaudi Afternoon,* Susan Seidelman (2001) – Judy Davis portrays a translator living in Barcelona in this flick about an American woman, Frankie, who asks Cassandra (played by Davis) to help her search for her husband, who has run away with their daughter and his lover.

> *Barcelona,* Whit Stillman (1994) – Two American cousins get tangled up in Barcelona, where love, politics and a little terrorism are the ingredients of this so-so film with some striking views of the city.

with Cubism and become one of the greatest artists of the 20th century. Continuing the burst of brilliance was the Barcelona-born surrealist Joan Miró (1893–1983), best remembered for his use of symbolic figures in primary colours.

Antoni Tàpies (b 1923), whose hallmark is the use of anything from sand to bits of furniture in his grand works, remains Barcelona's senior contemporary artistic icon today. See p169 for more on contemporary artists.

# DIRECTORY
## TRANSPORT
### ARRIVAL & DEPARTURE
### AIR

Most flights arrive at **Aeroport del Prat – Barcelona** ( ☎ 902 404704; www .aena.es), 12km southwest of the city centre. Some low-cost airlines, including Ryanair, use Girona-Costa Brava airport, 80km north of Barcelona.

#### Aeroport del Prat – Barcelona

The **A1 Aerobús** ( ☎ 93 415 60 20; €4.05) runs from the airport to Plaça de Catalunya (30 to 40 minutes) via Plaça d'Espanya and Gran Via de les Corts Catalanes every six to 15 minutes from 6am to 1am. Departures from Plaça de Catalunya are from 5.30am to 12.15am and go via Plaça d'Espanya. Buy tickets on the bus or from machines at the airport (if they are working!). Considerably slower local buses (such as bus 46 to/from Plaça d'Espanya and the N17 night bus to/from Plaça de Catalunya) also operate. You can use the T-10 multiride ticket (see Travel Passes, opposite) on all services.

Renfe's *rodalies* (local train) line C10 runs every half-hour between the airport and Estació de França (Map pp76–7, F5; about 35 minutes), stopping also at Estació Sants (the main train station; Map pp136–7, B1) and central Passeig de Gràcia. Tickets cost €2.60, unless you have a T-10 multiride ticket. The service from the airport starts at 6am.

A **taxi** ( ☎ 93 225 00 00, 93 300 11 00, 93 303 30 33) to/from the centre – about a half-hour ride depending on traffic – costs €18 to €22.

#### Girona-Costa Brava Airport

**Sagalés** ( ☎ 902 130014; www.sagales.com) runs hourly services from Girona-

---

### CLIMATE CHANGE & TRAVEL

Travel – especially by air – is a significant contributor to global climate change. At Lonely Planet, we believe that all who travel have a responsibility to limit their personal impact. We have teamed with Rough Guides and other concerned industry partners to support Climate Care, which allows people to offset the greenhouse gases they are responsible for with contributions to energy-saving projects and other climate-friendly initiatives in the developing world. Lonely Planet offsets all staff and author travel.

For more information, turn to the responsible travel pages on www.lonelyplanet.com. For details on offsetting your carbon emissions and a carbon calculator, go to www.climatecare.org.

## TAKE THE TRAIN!

Overnight trains run to Barcelona from Milan, Paris and Zürich – contact **Renfe** (www .renfe.es) for details. Plenty of high-speed trains also connect Barcelona with Madrid. From London, take the **Eurostar** (www.eurostar.com) to Paris and change there. If you leave in the morning, you could have lunch and an afternoon's sightseeing or shopping in Paris before climbing aboard the *Trenhotel* at Paris Austerlitz at 8.32pm (arriving in Barcelona at 8.24am). You can book this trip at www.raileurope.co.uk. Otherwise, high-speed TGV trains run regularly from Paris to Montpellier, from where direct services run to Barcelona (see www.voyages-sncf.com).

Costa Brava airport to Girona's main bus and train station (€2.05, 25 minutes) in connection with flights. The same company runs Barcelona Bus services to/from Estació Nord (Map pp106–7; G3) in Barcelona (one way/return €12/21, 70 minutes). A taxi to Barcelona would cost €120 or more.

## VISA

EU nationals require only their ID cards to live and work in Spain. Nationals of Bulgaria, Cyprus and Romania do not need visas for tourist visits but do not yet have the full freedom to live and work legally in Spain. Nationals of many other countries, including Australia, Canada, Israel, Japan, New Zealand and the USA, do not require visas for tourist visits of up to 90 days. Non EU nationals who are legal residents of one Schengen country do not require a visa to visit another Schengen country.

## GETTING AROUND

Barcelona has a user-friendly transport system. The efficient Metro stops close to most places of interest and is complemented by the suburban Ferrocarrils de la Generalitat de Catalunya (FGC) railway and an extensive bus network. In this book, the nearest Metro/bus/FGC stations or routes are noted after the Ⓜ / 🚌 / 🚆 symbols in each listing. The table on p188 lists the best options for getting to some of the main areas of interest.

## TRAVEL PASSES

*Targetes* are multiple-trip tickets that will save you time and money and are sold at most Metro stations. A T-10 (€7.20) gives you 10 trips on the Metro, buses and FGC trains; a T-DIA (€5.50) gives unlimited travel on all transport for one day. Two-/three-/four-/five-day tickets for unlimited travel on all transport except *rodalies* (local trains) cost €10/14.30/18.30/21.70.

## METRO & FGC

### Transports Metropolitans de Barcelona

(TMB; ☎ 010; www.tmb.net) runs a Metro system with six colour-coded lines. Single tickets, good for one journey no matter how many changes you have to make, cost €1.30 and can be bought at Metro stations. The Metro operates from 5am to midnight Sunday to Thursday, from 5am to 2am on Friday, and from 5am to 5am on Saturday and days immediately before main holidays.

The **FGC** ( ☎ 93 205 15 15; www.fgc.net) suburban rail network is handy for trips from Plaça de Catalunya to scattered attractions such as Tibidabo and Pedralbes. It operates on the same schedule as the Metro.

## BUS

**TMB buses** ( ☎ 010; www.tmb.net) run from 5am or 6am to as late as 11pm, depending on the line. Many routes pass through Plaça de Catalunya and/or Plaça de la Universitat. After 11pm a reduced network of yellow *nitbusos* (night buses) runs until 3am or 5am. All *nitbus* routes pass through Plaça de Catalunya and most run every 30 to 45 minutes. Single tickets cost €1.30 and are bought on the bus.

## RECOMMENDED MODES OF TRANSPORT

| | Park Güell | Passeig de Gràcia | La Sagrada Família |
|---|---|---|---|
| **Park Güell** | n/a | Metro + walk; 20min | Metro + walk; 30min |
| **Passeig de Gràcia** | Metro + walk; 20min | n/a | Metro + walk; 15min |
| **La Sagrada Família** | Metro + walk; 30min | Metro + walk; 15min | n/a |
| **Montjuïc** | funicular + Metro; 40-45min | funicular + Metro; 25-30min | funicular + Metro; 35-40min |
| **La Barceloneta** | Metro + bus + walk; 45min | Metro + walk; 25min | Metro + walk; 30min |
| **Tibidabo** | funicular + bus + walk + Metro; 55min | funicular + tram + Metro or bus; 60-70min | funicular + tram + Metro; 50-60min |
| **La Rambla** | Metro + walk; 25min | walk; 5-10min | walk + Metro; 20min |

## TAXI

Taxis are reasonably priced and charges are posted on passenger-side windows inside. The trip from Estació Sants to Plaça de Catalunya, about 3km, costs about €8. You can call a **taxi** (☎ 93 225 00 00, 93 300 11 00, 93 303 30 33, 93 322 22 22) or flag one down in the street.

## TRAM

**TMB** (☎ 902 193275; www.trambcn.com) runs three tram lines (T1, T2 and T3) into the suburbs of greater Barcelona from Plaça de Francesc Macià; these are of limited interest to visitors. The T4 line runs from behind the zoo near the Ciutadella Vila Olímpica Metro stop to Sant Adrià, via Glòries and El Fòrum. The T5 line runs from Glòries to Badalona. All standard transport passes are valid.

## TRIXIS

These three-wheeled **cycle taxis** (☎ 93 310 13 79; www.trixi.info) operate on the waterfront from 11am to 8pm daily, March to November. They can take two passengers and cost €10/18 per half-hour/hour. Children aged three to 12 pay half. You can find them near the Monument a Colom and in front of La Catedral.

| Montjuïc | La Barceloneta | Tibidabo | La Rambla |
| --- | --- | --- | --- |
| Metro + funicular; 40-45min | bus + Metro + walk; 45min | Metro + walk + bus + funicular; 55min | walk + Metro; 25min |
| Metro + funicular; 25-30min | Metro + walk; 25min | Metro + tram + funicular or bus; 60-70min | walk; 5-10min |
| Metro + funicular; 25-30min | Metro + walk; 30min | Metro + tram + funicular or bus; 60-70min | Metro + walk; 20min |
| n/a | funicular + Metro; 25-30min | funicular + Metro + tram + funicular or bus; 80min | funicular + Metro; 20-25min |
| Metro + funicular; 25-30min | n/a | Metro + tram + funicular or bus; 70-80min | Metro + walk; 25min |
| funicular + Metro + tram + funicular or bus; 80min | funicular + tram + Metro; 60-70min | n/a | funicular + tram + Metro or bus; 60-70min |
| Metro + funicular; 20-25min | Metro + walk; 25min | Metro + tram + funicular or bus; 60-70min | n/a |

# PRACTICALITIES
## BUSINESS HOURS

Folks in Barcelona work Monday to Friday from 8am or 9am to 2pm and then again from 4.30pm or 5pm for another three hours. Shops open from around 10am to 2pm and again from 4.30pm to 8.30pm Monday to Saturday; a growing number skip the lunch break. Department stores open from 10am to 10pm Monday to Saturday.

Banks tend to open from 8.30am to 2pm Monday to Friday. Some open again from around 4pm to 7pm on Thursday evenings, and/or on Saturday mornings from around 9am to 1pm. The **main post office** (Map pp76-7, D6; ☎ 902 197197; www.correos.es; Plaça d'Antoni López; Ⓜ Jaume I) opens from 8.30am to 10pm Monday to Saturday and from noon to 10pm on Sunday. Many other branches open from 8.30am to 2.30pm Monday to Friday and 9.30am to 1pm on Saturday.

Restaurants open for lunch from around 1.30pm to 4pm and reopen for dinner from 8pm to midnight; locals wouldn't dream of eating before 2pm and 9.30pm respectively. Pubs and bars generally open from around 8pm to 2am (to 3am Friday and Saturday); clubs stay open till 6am.

## DISCOUNTS

**Articket** (www.articketbcn.org) gives you admission to seven important art galleries, including the Museu Picasso and Museu Nacional d'Art de Catalunya (MNAC), for €20 and is valid for six months.

**ArqueoTicket** (€17) is for those with a special interest in ancient history. It gets you entry to the Museu Marítim, Museu d'Història de la Ciutat, Museu d'Arqueologia de Catalunya, Museu Egipci and Museu Barbier-Mueller d'Art Precolombí.

The **Barcelona Card** (www.barcelona card.com) costs €24/29/33/36 (a little less for children aged four to 12) for two/three/four/five days and could be worthwhile if you intend to cram in a lot. You get free transport (and 20% off the Aerobús) and discounted admission (up to 30% off) or free entry to many sights.

All cards are available at tourist offices.

The Ruta del Modernisme pack (see the boxed text, p105) is well worth looking into.

## HOLIDAYS

**New Year's Day** 1 January
**Epiphany** 6 January
**Good Friday** Late March/April
**Easter Monday** Late March/April
**Labour Day** 1 May
**Dilluns de Pasqua Grande** (day after Pentecost Sunday) May/June
**Feast of St John the Baptist** 24 June
**Feast of the Assumption** 15 August

**Catalonia's National Day** 11 September
**Festes de la Mercè** 24 September
**Spain's National Day** 12 October
**All Saints Day** 1 November
**Constitution Day** 6 December
**Feast of the Immaculate Conception**
8 December
**Christmas Day** 25 December
**St Stephen's Day** (Boxing Day) 26 December

## INTERNET

There are many internet centres in Barcelona. A growing number of hotels offer wi-fi access and/or high-speed modem access in rooms. A paying wi-fi service operates at the airport and train stations. City bars and restaurants are also latching on to wi-fi; the Fresh & Ready fast-food chain is one.

### INTERNET CAFES

Some internet centres offer student rates and also sell cards for several hours' use at reduced rates. A handful of options follows:
**Bornet** (Map pp76-7, D4; ☎ 93 268 15 07; Carrer de Barra Ferro 3; 1/10hr €2.80/20; ⏱ 10am-11pm Mon-Fri, noon-11pm Sat, Sun & holidays; Ⓜ Jaume I)
**easyInternetcafé** (www.easyeverything .com); Barri Gòtic (Map p43, B5; La Rambla 31; per hr €2.50; ⏱ 8am-2.30am; Ⓜ Liceu); l'Eixample (Map pp106-7, E5; ☎ 93 412 13 97; Ronda de l'Universitat 35; per hr €2.50; ⏱ 8am-2am; Ⓜ Universitat) The Barri Gòtic branch is upstairs from the Sports Bar.
**Internet MSN** (Map p129, C5; Carrer del Penedès 1; per min €0.02; ⏱ 9.30am-2am; Ⓜ Fontana)

## USEFUL WEBSITES

**Barcelona** (Barcelona Town Hall; www.bcn .cat) Has numerous links of general and tourist interest.
**Barcelona in Progress** (http://bcnip .blogsome.com in Spanish) A blog that captures swaths of news on Barcelona.
**Barcelona Turisme** (www.barcelonaturisme .com) The city's official tourism website.
**Barcelonareporter.com** (www.bar celonareporter.com) An English-language news site.
**BCN Nightlife** (www.bcn-nightlife.com) Info on bars, clubs and parties.
**Le Cool** (http://lecool.com) A free weekly guide to what's happening in Barcelona.
**Ruta del Modernisme** (www.rutadel modernisme.com) A specific site on Modernisme in Barcelona.

## LANGUAGE

Barcelona is a bilingual city, with all locals speaking Catalan and Spanish. Many people from elsewhere in Spain speak Spanish only. A growing number of people speak at least some English. No one expects you to learn Catalan, but a few words of Spanish can go a long way. Where necessary, the masculine and feminine endings (usually 'o' and 'a', respectively) for words and phrases are given here.

### BASICS

| | |
|---|---|
| Hello. | ¡Hola! |
| Goodbye. | ¡Adiós! |
| Yes. | Sí. |

| No. | No. |
| Please. | Por favor. |
| Thank you. | Gracias. |
| You're welcome. | De nada. |
| Excuse me. | Perdón. |
| Sorry/ Excuse me. | Lo siento/ Discúlpeme. |
| Do you speak English? | ¿Habla inglés? |
| I don't understand. | No entiendo. |
| How much is this? | ¿Cuánto vale esto? |
| Where are the toilets? | ¿Dónde están los servicios? |

## GETTING AROUND

Where is the Metro station?
  *¿Dónde está la parada de Metro?*
I want to go to…
  *Quiero ir a…*
Can you show me (on the map)?
  *¿Me puede indicar (en el plano)?*
When does the…leave/arrive?
  *¿A qué hora sale/llega el…?*

| bus | autobús/bus |
| Metro | Metro |
| train | tren |

## AROUND TOWN

I'm looking for…
  *Estoy buscando…*

| a bank | un banco |
| the cathedral | la catedral |
| the hospital | el hospital |
| the police | la policía |

## EATING

| breakfast | desayuno |
| lunch | comida/ almuerzo |
| dinner | cena |
| I'd like the set menu. | Quisiera el menú del día. |
| I'm a vegetarian. | Soy vegetariano/a. |

## TIME, DAYS & NUMBERS

| What time is it? | ¿Qué hora es? |
| today | hoy |
| tomorrow | mañana |
| yesterday | ayer |
| morning | mañana |
| afternoon | tarde |
| evening | noche |

| Monday | lunes |
| Tuesday | martes |
| Wednesday | miércoles |
| Thursday | jueves |
| Friday | viernes |
| Saturday | sábado |
| Sunday | domingo |

| 0 | cero |
| 1 | uno/una |
| 2 | dos |
| 3 | tres |
| 4 | cuatro |
| 5 | cinco |
| 6 | seis |
| 7 | siete |
| 8 | ocho |
| 9 | nueve |
| 10 | diez |
| 100 | cien/ciento |
| 1000 | mil |

## EMERGENCIES

| Help! | ¡Socorro! |
|-------|-----------|
| Call a doctor! | ¡Llame a un médico! |
| Call the police! | ¡Llame a la policía! |
| I'm lost. | Me he perdido/a. |

## MONEY

### CURRENCY

Spain's currency is the euro. **Interchange** (Map p43, A4; ☎ 93 342 73 11; La Rambla dels Caputxins 74; ⏰ 9am-10.30pm; Ⓜ Liceu) is centrally located and represents American Express. For exchange rates at the time of publication, see the inside front cover.

### COSTS

Locals complain that prices (but not wages) are rapidly approaching those of other major European centres. That is not entirely true. Cocktails can easily cost €8 to €10 nowadays, but a set lunch can still be had for under €10. Public transport and taxis remain cheaper than just about anywhere else in Europe. Many museums have free admission days.

Average daily costs depend greatly on your activities. On a tight budget, you could get by on about €50 to €60 a day in dorm accommodations, eating a set lunch and snacking in the evening. A more realistic midrange budget for a modest hotel room, three square meals a day, a museum and a drink or two would be closer to €100 to €120 a day.

## NEWSPAPERS & MAGAZINES

The national, slightly left-of-centre *El País* includes a daily supplement devoted to Catalonia. *La Vanguardia* (with a good listings magazine on Friday) and *El Periódico* are the main local Spanish-language dailies. Catalan dailies include *Avui* (conservative and Catalan-nationalist-oriented) and *El Punt* (concentrating on news in and around Barcelona). A plethora of international press is available at main central-city newsstands, especially along La Rambla.

The city's tourist board publishes *Barcelona – The Official Gay and Lesbian Tourist Guide* biannually. The free biweekly *Shanguide*, jammed with listings and contact ads, is sometimes available in gay bookshops. Magazines available in gay bookshops include *Nois* ('boys' in Catalan) and *Gay Barcelona*. The annual, worldwide *Spartacus* guide is often on sale at newsstands along La Rambla.

## ORGANISED TOURS

The **Oficina d'Informació de Turisme de Barcelona** (Map p63, C2; ☎ 93 285 38 34; Plaça de Catalunya 17-S; Ⓜ Catalunya) organises guided walking tours that explore the Barri Gòtic; follow in Picasso's footsteps (including the Museu Picasso); observe the main jewels of Modernisme; and take in traditional purveyors of fine foodstuffs, from chocolate to sausages, across the old city. All tours last around two hours and start at the tourist office, where you can find out the latest timetables. They cost €11 to €15 for adults, €4.50 to €6.50 for children.

## TELEPHONE

Telefónica phonecards for payphones can be purchased in €6 and €12 denominations from tobacconists and post offices. Cut-rate phonecards for cheap international calls are also available from many tobacconists and some newsstands.

## MOBILE PHONES

Spain uses the GSM cellular phone system, compatible with phones sold in the rest of Europe, Australia and most of Asia, but not those from North America and Japan (unless you have a tri-band or quad-band handset). Check with your service provider that it has a roaming agreement with a local counterpart, which can be expensive. You can buy pay-as-you-go SIM cards from local providers for around €10, useful provided your phone is unblocked.

## COUNTRY & CITY CODES

The city code (including the leading 9) is an integral part of the number and must always be dialled, whether calling from next door or abroad.

| | | |
|---|---|---|
| **Spain country code** | ☎ | 34 |
| **Barcelona city code** | ☎ | 93 |

## USEFUL PHONE NUMBERS

| | | |
|---|---|---|
| **International access code** | ☎ | 00 |
| **International directory inquiries** | ☎ | 11825 |
| **International operator and reverse charges (collect)** | | |
| Europe | ☎ | 1008 |
| rest of world | ☎ | 1005 |
| **Local directory inquiries** | ☎ | 11818 |

## TIPPING

You are not expected to tip on top of restaurant service charges, but it is common to leave a small amount, say €1 per person. If there is no service charge, a 5% to 10% tip is optional. In bars, locals often leave some small change (€0.05 to €0.10). Tipping taxi drivers is not common practice, but you should tip the porter (€1 to €2) at higher-class hotels.

## TOURIST INFORMATION

In addition to the following tourist offices, several information booths operate at least through the summer. The main tourist office can help with finding accommodation.

**Oficina d'Informació de Turisme de Barcelona** (www.barcelonaturisme.com); main office (Map p63, C2; ☎ 93 285 38 32; Plaça de Catalunya 17-S, underground; ⏰ 9am-9pm; Ⓜ Catalunya); Aeroport del Prat (Terminals A & B arrivals halls; ⏰ 9am-9pm); Barri Gòtic (Map p43, C3; Carrer de la Ciutat 2; ⏰ 9am-8pm Mon-Fri, 10am-8pm Sat, 10am-2pm Sun & holidays; Ⓜ Jaume I); Estació Sants (Map pp136-7, B1; ⏰ 8am-8pm daily Jun-Sep, 8am-8pm Mon-Fri, to 2pm Sat, Sun & holidays Oct-May; Ⓜ Sants Estació)

**Palau de la Virreina arts information office** (Map p43, A3; ☎ 93 301 77 75; La Rambla de Sant Josep 99; ⏰ 10am-8pm; Ⓜ Liceu) A useful office for events information and tickets.

**Palau Robert regional tourist office** (Map pp106-7, C3; ☎ 93 238 80 91; www .gencat.net/probert; Passeig de Gràcia 107; ⏰ 10am-7pm Mon-Sat, to 2.30pm Sun; Ⓜ Diagonal)

## TRAVELLERS WITH DISABILITIES

Some hotels, monuments and public institutions have wheelchair access. All Metro stations should be wheelchair-adapted (with lifts) by 2012. Buses already are. Many road crossings have been made wheelchair-friendly in recent years. Crossing lights are adapted for the sight-impaired. **Taxi Amic** ( ☎ 93 420 80 88; www .terra.es/personal/taxiamic in Spanish) is a special taxi service for those with disabilities.

**Accessible Barcelona** ( ☎ 93 428 52 27; www.accessiblebarcelona.com) is run by Craig Grimes, a T6 paraplegic and inveterate traveller. Hotels are well researched and the company will help with transport and other aspects of your trip.

# >INDEX

*See also separate subindexes for See (p203), Shop (p205), Eat (p206), Drink (p207) and Play (p208).*

## ◎ SEE

000 map pages

🍴 **EAT**

**000** map pages